D0987255

THE LIBRARY
ST. MARY'S COLLEGE OF MARYLAND.
ST. MARY'S CITY. MARYLAND 20686

Pacifism
and the Just War

Pacifism
and the Just War

A Study in Applied Philosophy

Jenny Teichman

Basil Blackwell

© Jenny Teichman 1986

First published 1986

Basil Blackwell Ltd
108 Cowley Road, Oxford OX4 1JF, UK

Basil Blackwell Inc.
432 Park Avenue South, Suite 1503,
New York, NY 10016, USA

All rights reserved. Except for the quotation of short passages for the purposes of criticism and review, no part of this publication may be reproduced, stored in a retrieval system, or transmitted, in any form or by any means, electronic, mechanical, photocopying, recording or otherwise, without the prior permission of the publisher.

Except in the United States of America, this book is sold subject to the condition that it shall not, by way of trade or otherwise, be lent, re-sold, hired out, or otherwise circulated without the publisher's prior consent in any form of binding or cover other than that in which it is published and without a similar condition including this condition being imposed on the subsequent purchaser.

British Library Cataloguing in Publication Data

Teichman, Jenny
  Pacifism and the just war: a study
  in applied philosophy.
  1. Just war doctrine   2. Pacifism
  I. Title
  261.8'73   U21.2
  ISBN 0–631–15056–0

Library of Congress Cataloging in Publication Data

Teichman, Jenny.
  Pacifism and the just war.

  Bibliography: p.
  Includes index.
  1. Pacifism—Religious aspects—Christianity.
2. Pacifism. 3. Just war doctrine. I. Title.
BT736.4.T45 1986 241'.6242 86–8244
ISBN 0–631–15056–0

Typeset by Cambrian Typesetters, Frimley, Surrey
Printed in Great Britain by Billing & Sons Limited, Worcester

To my brother, Michael

Contents

Acknowledgements

I am very indebted to Professor Peter Brock, of the University of Toronto. Firstly, because his several books on the history of pacifism must surely be essential sources of information to anyone who is interested in that subject. Secondly, because Professor Brock was kind enough to read the manuscript of the present work and to point out errors and suggest improvements. I am most grateful to him for this; and I wish to inform readers that any historical blunders remaining in the text are all my own work.

In chapter nine and in the first part of chapter four I have borrowed and adapted ideas taken from three papers by C. A. J. Coady, of the University of Melbourne. I wish to thank Tony Coady for his generosity in allowing me to use this material, and for lending me copies of his papers before they had appeared in print.

Finally, I would like to thank Mr Nicholas Denyer, of Trinity College Cambridge, Dr. A. J. P. Kenny, of Balliol College Oxford, Mrs Mary Midgley, of the University of Newcastle and Dr M. A. Stewart, of the University of Lancaster, each of whom made various helpful suggestions about the form or the content of this book.

Acknowledgements

Introduction

Pacifism is in part a code of conduct but it is also a theory or set of theories about the moral status of war. Its most important philosophical rival is the traditional doctrine of the just war.

The chief purposes of this book are to describe and analyse the theses of pacifism and the doctrines of the just war theory; to compare them with each other; and to consider the objections that have been made or might be made against each and against both.

In the first three chapters I give an account of pacifism which is partly descriptive and partly analytic.

Chapter four considers various definitions of violence, and refutes the supposed objection to pacifism that its thesis is self-contradictory.

In chapter five I discuss another objection to pacifism, namely, that warfare is the same sort of thing as the control of crime and in itself is not more immoral than ordinary police actions.

Chapter six contains an account of the traditional theory of the just war which is partly descriptive and historical and partly analytic.

Chapter seven examines objections to the effect that the theory of the just war rests on incoherent notions of guilt and innocence, in particular, the objection that the ordinary distinction between innocence and guilt, when applied to warfare, generates an inconsistent triad of propositions.

In chapter eight I analyse the concept of self-defence and attempt to refute the idea that violence, even when used in self-defence, cannot be justified.

Chapter nine defines *terrorism*, and considers the theoretical problems posed by terrorism for pacifism and for the theory of the just war.

In chapter ten I attempt to answer the following questions: Are there any intrinsically good states of affairs or actions? Are there any intrinsically evil states of affairs or actions? Does *intrinsic* mean the same as *essential*? Do intrinsic goods and evils generate absolute obligations? Must pacifism, and/or the doctrines of the just war, be thought of as entailing a theory of absolute obligation? Is war intrinsically evil?

There are two appendices. The first consists of a selection of extracts from writings by philosophers and others on the topic of war. These have been chosen because, as it seems to me, they are interesting and thought-provoking. Of course there are many other possible selections which would have been equally interesting and thought-provoking, but this short appendix is not intended as a representative anthology of thoughts about war. The second appendix consists of some reflections on the moral status of deterrent threats.

1

The Meaning of Pacifism

The word *pacifism* is relatively new, dating from the beginning of this century. The *Complete Oxford Dictionary* published in 1904 does not contain the term, which was added in the Supplement of 1982, although the various shorter versions of the *O.E.D.* do contain the word in editions before 1982. Its first appearance is recorded by the Supplement as having occurred in 1902 when it was used, or coined, by a Frenchman attending an international peace congress. He said that by *pacifism* he meant *anti-war-ism*. In *The Times* of 30 July 1906 the word appeared again, this time in inverted commas. In 1915 the *National Review* stated 'the greatest war in history is now being fought in the cause of pacifism', by which it meant, presumably, the cause of a lasting peace rather than the cause of a wholesale rejection of war as such. The *O.E.D.* Supplement also quotes from *The Baltimore Sun* of 1930. This newspaper castigated 'pacifists and defeatists'.

The rejection of war is often coupled with treason in the public mind. Thus G. B. Shaw, writing about public attitudes to war during 1914–18 in the Preface to *Heartbreak House*, remarks 'There was only one virtue, pugnacity, and only one vice, pacifism'.[1]

Pacifism is not a single unitary theory about war and peace but rather a collection of related theories. In other words, there are different varieties of pacifism. Too many twentieth century philosophers who have attacked (or defended) pacifism have failed to see this.

An 'ism' word may name a type of action (as, baptism), or a kind of trait (as, alcoholism), or a state of affairs (as, barbarism), or a system of practice (as, vegetarianism, monasticism). Or an 'ism' word may be the name of a single unitary theory (as, positivism, Calvinism, monetarism). Finally, it can be the name of a set of theories which have something in common. *Realism*, for instance, refers to a whole group of philosophical theories; hence a philosopher can be a realist in regard to some entities and an anti-realist in regard to others. To take another example, *paganism*, *monotheism* and *polytheism* are all names for classes of religions; thus monotheism is a class which contains four major religions, namely Judaism, Christianity, Islam and Sikhism.

Although the word 'pacifism' is fairly new it has been predicated retrospectively of many sects and movements, particularly of religious groups such as the Quakers and the Mennonites, but also of some non-religious ones such as the Anarchists, for these too refuse to allow that the State has a right to conscript for war. Thus for various reasons we must conclude that the term *pacifism* is more like *realism* or *monotheism* than like (say) *vegetarianism* or *Calvinism*.

Let us therefore take *pacifism* to be the name of a set of theories or beliefs which have as a common feature opposition to war: I shall call it 'anti-war-ism', choosing this name for the reasons already given.

Next it is necessary to distinguish pacifism from (on the one hand) love of peace pure and simple, and (on the other hand) pragmatic attempts to abolish war. Pacifism can also be distinguished from opposition to all forms of violence as such.

All sane people prefer peace to war, I suppose, but their reasons are various and not all are aptly described as pacifist in character. A rational preference for peace is quite consistent with a belief that war is a necessary evil, perhaps an absolutely necessary evil. Occasionally one hears the view that only a soldier can really understand the value of peace – that is, the view that military men are the real pacifists. Such a notion is sometimes tied up with a defence of the value of deterrent threats directed at potential enemies, i.e., with the theory that if you want peace it is essential to prepare for war; or with the vaguely high-minded proposition that peace is not 'merely' the absence of war but rather 'a positive state of mind' (whatever that may be).

Furthermore some love of peace or attachment to peace is professional or vocational. For instance, Buddhist monks are forbidden to shed animal or human blood and they are forbidden, of course, as a result, to take part in warfare. They are not so much as allowed to watch battles, or even mock-battles. But Buddhist laymen, according to some varieties of this religion, are permitted to become soldiers. And Buddhists (again, according to some views) may eat animal flesh provided the animal was killed by a non-Buddhist butcher. Christian priests may not shed human blood but themselves sometimes argue and teach that it is all right for Christian laymen to go to war. Vocational pacifism, then, can, but need not, go with anti-war-ism.

Pragmatic attempts to abolish or reduce war need not necessarily stem from strong feelings of moral repugnance about war. There may be simply a judgement that war is wasteful, or bad for trade, or something of that kind. A. J. P. Taylor coined the word *pacificism* as a general descriptive term designed to cover all the different attempts made (for any reason) to abolish war, and we can contrast this idea with that of pacifism proper, which involves being against war on more then merely pragmatic grounds. Pacifism proper involves a moral judgement and a personal commitment. This is true of all varieties of pacifism. Naturally all pacifists are pacificists, but not all pacificists are pacifists.

It is also necesary to distinguish pacifism proper from a more wide-ranging opposition to violence. Pacifism is not the view that all violence whatsoever is wrong unconditionally. Certainly some pacifist sects reject not only the violence of armies and warfare but also the lesser violence of police forces, schoolmasters, etc. Since much pacifism has a Christian basis many pacifists believe that it is right to 'turn the other cheek' both in the community and in international disputes. Eastern pacifism such as that espoused by Ghandi teaches that it is always wrong to meet violence with violence and that it is always wrong to kill. The arguments of some early Christians, St Augustine for example, do not always differentiate between oposition to violence as such, and opposition to war; when they do it is chiefly in order to argue that there is in fact no significant difference here. Thus Augustine argues that punishment and war are essentially similar. Modern philosophers writing on war and pacifism also seem to take it for granted that opposition to war must involve or even entail opposition to all violence directed against human beings.

There are two reasons for rejecting the notion that pacifism is just the same thing as opposition to violence *per se*. The first reason is simply that the very word *pacifism* was coined to mean *anti-war-ism*: as such it is a useful word with a relatively precise meaning which it is best not to blur or abolish. Secondly, the groups of people who are retrospectively described as pacifists, or who today describe themselves as pacifists, are not by any means all committed to a rejection of every possible type of violence. What they have in common is a principled rejection of the violence of war. Some, it is true, are also opposed to 'the violence of the magistrate': but that is not the essence of pacifism. Some, and more than a few if we include Indian pacifists, believe it is wrong to eat the flesh of animals; all the same, vegetarianism is not the same thing as pacifism, nor is it logically entailed by pacifism. In short, just as it is possible to be a pacifist without being a vegetarian, so it is possible to be a pacifist without being committed to a total rejection of violence in all circumstances. Many proofs (so-called) of the incoherence of pacifism depend on making the assumption that anyone who is anti-war must be and will be against all kinds of physical force in all situations.

The common core of pacifist doctrine is a principled

rejection of war. But the (moral or religious) principles which dictate a refusal to shed human blood in warfare are themselves quite various. To begin with, pacifism may be conditional or unconditional. Conditional pacifism in turn splits up into different kinds, depending on the conditions which make it conditional. Well then, what kinds of conditional pacifism are possible? Here are some examples. Some Christians have believed that although war was permissible in Old Testament times it ceased to be allowable after the new teaching of Jesus. Again, there are many people today who regard themselves as pacifists who argue that, although war might have been all right once when weapons were, in the main, of the kind used to kill combatants and when soldiers did in fact mainly kill each other, it is no longer the same kind of activity when the weapons used will kill huge numbers of civilians: since it is no longer the same kind of activity, since it has become what it has become, it is no longer possible to justify it. Or again there are those who believe that, while war might be morally permissible if those who engage in it are all volunteers, it is not morally permissible when all or many or most of those who engage in it are impressed or conscripted, possibly under threat of execution if they resist. And since modern war has to date been mostly carried out with conscript armies it follows that modern warfare is not morally permissible according to this view. These last two varieties of conditional pacifism might well be called *just war pacifisms* for they exemplify the idea that war, or most war, or modern war, because of its very nature, cannot possibly fulfil those canons of justice which were supposed to make the activity all right. A just war, or a just modern war, is for such pacifists a concept rather like the concept of an absolutely perfect sinless human being. The concept makes sense, it is not exactly a contradiction in terms, yet the nature of the beast is such that we can say with certainty that the logical possibility is never going to be realized. So even if there exists a coherent doctrine of justice in war that makes no odds: no actual wars can be justified.

It would not do to try to analyse the nature of some subject or pursuit – philosophy, say – without taking into account what its practitioners – philosophers, for instance – have said: for after all philosophy must have something to do with what philosophers believe themselves to be doing. Similarly it would be unwise to try to analyse a theory or set of beliefs such as pacifism while ignoring what those whose theory it is have to say. In order to avoid this mistake, and also to avoid the appearance of relying too heavily on the dictionary and on my own intuitions, I will end this chapter with a discussion of what has been said by two pacifists about the nature of pacifism.

Peter Brock is an historian of pacifism whose works trace the history of pacifist movements in the USA, England, and Europe. In his writings *pacifism* and *war-resistance* are closely linked and often come to much the same thing.[2]

Brock describes a number of types of pacifism, as follows:

Vocational pacifism is the pacifism of priests and others in holy orders. It can (though it need not) go with anti-war-ism or with theories about non-violence.

Eschatological pacifism is an interim ethic which teaches that there will be an Apocalyptic war at the last day between the forces of good and evil, but until then wars are to be utterly rejected. Merely human wars, that is, are forbidden, and human beings will only be indirectly involved in the war of the Day of God's Wrath.

Separational pacifism is the view that the redeemed or favoured of God must separate themselves from the rest of mankind. Ordinary human society is irredeemably wicked and worldly so whoever wants to be saved must abandon it. The New Testament is taken as the Law, replacing the teaching of the Old Testament. War is condemned absolutely, but 'the violence of the magistrate' is accepted as conditionally justified; even that violence, however, is regarded as belonging in its essence to the realm of evil.

Integrational pacifism is the title given by Brock to those pacifist groups which combine an ethic of peace and peace-seeking with the setting up of reform movements whose platforms include opposition to war but may contain other aims as well, e.g. the abolition of racial segregation. Integrational pacifists do not reject government nor the use of force by government; they reject only the injurious use of external force in international relations. Modern Quakerism, in Brock's view, is an example of an integrational pacifist movement.

Goal-directed pacifism involves the use of non-violent techniques in order to achieve specific aims. Ghandi's fasting while in gaol is an example. Bertrand Russell's 'Direct Action', associated with his membership of 'The Committee of 100' in the 1950s, is another, the action in question being non-violent, e.g., sitting down in front of buildings inhabited by the Ministry of Defence. No doubt the Greenham Common Women are involved in goal-directed pacifism by this definition.

Brock's implicit taxonomy allows some overlapping but it throws light on our subject all the same. It draws attention, of course, to the fact that several varieties of belief are rightly called *pacifist*. And it is significant that Brock simply assumes without argument that the feature which different types of pacifism have in common is opposition to war.

John Yoder is a Mennonite professor of theology. He divides pacifism more or less according to its motivations, as follows.[3]

Firstly *the Christian claim to be a universal church* entails that Christianity has no special loyalty to any one nation or race or group. Since it has adherents in all nations it cannot take sides in conflicts between nations. This view of a universal religion, says Yoder, provides Christians with a basis for rejecting war absolutely.

Just war pacifism entails examining each case of armed conflict to see if it conforms to the conditions of justice in and for war. There is a rational presumption, because of the destructiveness of the activity of warfare, against any war's being just rather than unjust. So no government has a right to compel its citizens to fight: it falls to the individual's powers of moral judgement to determine whether fighting is all right in any case.

Absolute pacifism teaches that all deliberate killing of human beings is intrinsically evil.

Pragmatic pacifism, or political pacifism, is the theory that a refusal to fight will eventually solve the problem of war and is in fact the only way in which this problem can be solved.

Gandhian non-violence, which is a generalized form of political pacifism, sees non-violence, techniques of peaceful resistance, and conscientious objection as means towards solving not only the problem of war between nations but other political problems as well. These include the abuse of police powers, colonialism and racism. It regards techniques of non-violent resistance as the only resource (or, perhaps, the only non-self-defeating resource) open to weaker parties and oppressed groups. There can be, too, says Yoder, a kind of pacifism which involves an *absolute rejection of war* but not an *absolute rejection of all violence* or even of *all killing*.

There can be pacifism founded on *a new standard of righteousness*, the standard found in the New Testament.

Utopian pacifism is the idea that rejection of violence is the road to Utopia.

The pacifism of a categorical imperative is the theory that one is bound to adopt a maxim of behaviour which one can will to be a universal law of nature.

There can be pacifism based on an appeal to an *absolute conscience*: though unfortunately it is not very clear what Yoder means by this term; his idea of conscience would seem to be as of a still small voice that speaks but does not reason.

There can be a pacifism based on the belief that *political change is impossible* and that only *personal change* should be sought.

Yoder's categories overlap, but from our point of view this is less important than the fact that his list reminds us of the different kinds of religious or moral reasons that can lie behind characteristic pacifist practices such as non-violent resistance. And again the common feature of these pacifisms is anti-war-ism.

2

The Origins of Pacifism

The idea that war must be renounced comes to us from Christianity. The serious rejection of war as such, in contrast to a more general rejection of violence, does not appear before the Christian era. It is true, of course, that Buddhism condemns all killing, even of animals. But this is too wide a condemnation to count as anti-war-ism. Buddhist teaching, according to one interpretation, is that it is better to be killed by a wild animal – a snake, say – than to kill it first in self-defence. An extreme antipathy to the taking of life is also found in certain Hindu writings. It is characteristic of Jainism too. Jains do not eat flesh and some Hindu sects are vegetarian. Furthermore, one can find accounts of vocational pacifism in the scriptures of these religions. But the very strong traditions of personal and vocational non-violence in Hinduism, Buddhism and Jainism are not the same as pacifism when this is understood as essentially anti-war-ism.

Peter Brock says that there is no known instance of non-vocational conscientious objection to participation in war and no recorded advocacy of such objection before the Christian era. He further claims that until the nineteenth century pacifism in the West was confined to those who stood within the Christian tradition. Pacifism as we understand it was not found in any of the pagan religions of Africa, nor is it found in Islam, nor, as we have seen, is it an explicit part even of those non-violent sects of the Indian sub-continent and the Far East.[1]

It cannot be said that explicit anti-militarism is part and parcel of Christianity, and certainly not of institutional Christianity, yet it is characteristic of Christianity in that until quite recently probably most of those who proclaimed themselves pacifists were in fact members of Christian sects. Only a minority of Christians have been pacifists but most of the pacifists who have existed and have called themselves such, or have been called such, have either been Christians or have been strongly influenced by Christianity.

The doctrines of pacifism in the West are based firstly on various passages in the Gospels, secondly on what is taken to be the general tone of Christ's teachings, and thirdly on the fact of his own non-resistance to the Roman forces and the Jews who condemned him. Pacifist doctrines are expressed at least incipiently in the writings or the reported sayings of the early Christians. After the conversion of Constantine, Christianity lost its pacifist leanings, partly perhaps because of the urgency of the Emperor's wars against the barbarians.

In the Middle Ages and later, various heretic sects adopted anti-war doctrines. Pacifism is a characteristic form of 'renewal' for Christianity. There are some indications that Christianity today, even in its most institutionalized forms, is returning to a kind of pacifism.

Under the Romans Christianity was for a time a religion of Jews and women, people not eligible for military service. So it is difficult to infer their attitudes from their actions. On the other hand those who converted to the new religion included men who were already soldiers. Secondly, some of the early Fathers of the Church wrote about war and military service. Tertullian, for instance, writes 'How will a Christian make war – nay, how will he serve as a soldier, even in time of peace, without the sword, which the Lord has taken away?'.[2] Origen compares Christians generally with the priests of other religions, to whom the shedding of blood was forbidden. Christians, he says, should be exempted from military service.[3]

According to Brock, the early collections of legislation made in Christian communities in the first and second centuries AD rule that after baptism soldiers must leave the army. He also suggests that the intense persecution of Christians which was going on in the decades before the conversion of Constantine may have been in part a reaction to the fact that these increasingly numerous citizens refused to take part in the defence of Rome against the barbarians.[4]

In the fourth century the Synod of Arles ruled that a soldier who laid down his arms in peace time would be excommunicated. This ruling is cited by pacifists as proving that the Synod regarded peace-time soldiering (i.e., police work) as a duty and war-time soldiering as forbidden. That is, it is argued that the Synod was in fact opposed to war-time soldiering and assumed that it was already forbidden to Christians. Otherwise why should peace-time soldiers be specifically picked out for excommunication? But anti-pacifists argue that the Synod's reference has the force of 'even in peace time a soldier must not lay down his arms – still less in time of war'.

Some early saints refused to serve in armies. St Maximilianus of Numidia was required to join the Roman army because he was the son of a soldier. He refused and the authorities pointed out to him that other Christians were already serving. 'What wrong do these Christians do?' he was asked. He replied 'Thou knowest what wrong they do'. Maximilianus was executed in 295 AD. In 356 another saint, St Martin of Tours, threw down his arms on the eve of a battle. When he was accused of cowardice he said he would go into the battlefield unarmed. Some authors argue that Martin's action was, as it were, vocational in character, the result, not of being a Christian, but of his desire to become a monk; now from the fact that monks are forbidden to shed blood we may not infer that laymen are also forbidden to do so. But other authors think that Martin threw down his arms because of a conviction that no Christian should engage in war.

After these early times the Church adopted on the whole the teaching of St Augustine on war and peace. Briefly it is that war is akin to punishment. Punishment by the State – the 'violence of the magistrate' – is not unlawful; furthermore punishment as such is not incompatible with love, since parents lovingly chastise their children. A Christian Emperor (says Augustine) has a duty to fight against barbarians and God will support his cause if he does. Between the ninth and the thirteenth centuries scholars developed the theory of the just war, the point of which, of course, is to justify at least some wars.

While the Catholic Church was developing the just war theory, anti-war-ism appeared amongst those described as heretics. As examples we can mention the sect known as the Bohemian Brethren, and that other more famous one called Waldensians, both of which preached non-resistance to armed force. In England in 1395 the Lollards' petition to Parliament contained these words 'Manslaughter by battle or by law . . . is contrary to the New Testament unless it is justified by express revelation.'[5] Certain express revelations of the Old Testament exemplify the conditions which make war right according to a rather special kind of conditional pacifism: according to this type of pacifism, war is allowed only to those who have been directly commanded to fight by the voice of God himself, as Joshua was commanded.

Reforming sects like the Anabaptists and the Mennonites in the sixteenth century (who rejected 'the violence of the magistrate'), and the Quakers in the seventeenth century (who did not), adopted pacifism – that is, anti-war-ism – as a tenet of their Christian faith.

Pacifists of all varieties have commented on the fact that Christians when fighting Christians have chaplains who pray for the victory of one side or the other. Much the same thing happens when one Islamic nation fights another, each has many mullahs to claim national holiness. Non-believers, pacifist or not as the case may be, point out that the clergy sometimes show regrettable lack of immunity to the secular passions of nationalism.

However, there are some signs that the major branches of

the Christian Church in the late twentieth century are becoming increasingly sympathetic towards pacifist ideas. One symptom is a big shift in Catholic ideas about conscientious objection.

In 1957 Pope Pius XII wrote, 'A Catholic citizen may not appeal to his conscience as grounds for refusing to serve and fulfil duties fixed by law if the decision to undertake military operations is reached by freely elected leaders and there is express danger of unjust attack.'[6] Again, according to the *New Catholic Encyclopedia*, published in the USA in the 1960s, conscientious objection to army service is 'morally indefensible'.[6] This hard line might perhaps rest in part on the thesis that the ordinary citizen is not usually in a position to know whether his state is acting justly or unjustly in declaring war. After all, it is nowadays apparently believed by many politicians that their more important decisions, including of course those about war and peace, need secrecy if they are to succeed. Possibly the thought behind the Church's most recently expressed hostility to conscientious objection was that while citizens can know, perhaps, whether their government was properly elected, they have no means of knowing much about its international policies and intentions. Yet it is obvious, surely, that justice in elections is no guarantee of justice in international affairs.

However, the traditional (and repeated) condemnation of conscientious objection was not upheld by the Second Vatican Council of 1965. The Council stated 'It seems just that the law should make provision for the case of conscientious objectors who refuse to carry arms' and 'We cannot but express our admiration for all who forgo the use of violence to vindicate their rights and resort to those other means of defence which are available to weaker parties.' The doctrine that presupposition of right lies with the legitimate authorities was also not upheld by the Council, which decided 'People should beware of leaving these problems [i.e., those of war and disarmament] to the efforts of a few men for . . . state leaders rely to a large extent on public opinion and public attitudes'.[7] Another shift is apparent in the attitude towards the right of self-defence. In 1953 Pope Pius XII wrote 'the right to be prepared for self-defence cannot be denied even in these days to any State'.[8] In the absence of any special qualifications, the right he referred to must surely be interpreted as involving the use of armed force. The Vatican Council's expressed admiration for those who resort to 'other means of defence' has already been noted: it was taken up by the (American) National Conference of Catholic Bishops in their statement *The Challenge of Peace*, issued from Chicago in 1983, in which they said 'Armed force is not the only defence against unjust aggression.'[9]

These shifts in the official teaching of a major segment of the Christian Church are surely not accidental, but rather stem from a new perception of international problems which has led to a deliberate attempt to re-think the whole question of war. This attempt began, perhaps, with Pope John XXIII's encyclical letter *Pacem in Terris* of 1963 in which he wrote 'In this age of ours which prides itself upon its atomic power it is irrational to think that war is a proper way to obtain justice for violated rights.' The Council document of 1965 adds to this 'the development of armaments by modern science has immeasurably magnified the horrors and wickedness of war. Warfare conducted by these weapons can inflict immense and indiscriminate havoc which goes far beyond the bounds of legitimate defence . . . these factors force us to undertake a completely fresh reappraisal of war' and 'Providence urgently demands of us that we free ourselves from the age-old slavery of war'.[10]

3

Pacifism and Conscription

It has been argued that 'without conscription pacifism is a private opinion'.[1] But this would appear to confuse pacifism with conscientious objection. Although pacifism requires from its adherents a commitment to refuse to give military service, its doctrines do not in general presuppose the existence of conscription. Furthermore it is possible to be a conscientious objector – for example by objecting to one particular war – without being a pacifist. Pacifism is not to be identified with the (essentially public) activity of refusing to serve in an army, but it is not essentially a private matter either. Pacifists and pacifist movements have made many public attempts to influence the policies of nations by propaganda, by parliamentary action, by peaceful protests and by direct appeals to heads of states. There is plenty of evidence for this in the history of Quakerism and indeed in today's newspapers.

There are many different kinds of armed force. Some military forces are made up of volunteers, others of conscripts, yet others of a mixture of professional volunteer leaders (officers) and conscripted or impressed part-time or temporary other ranks. Militia forces are generally defensive, part-time and conscripted. Professional standing armies may be local and defensive, or offensive and marauding, or either at different times and in different wars. Armies may be made up mainly of natives or chiefly of foreign mercenaries.

Some societies have lived by a kind of perpetual war or marauding. The hordes of Ghengis Khan lived like this and so too did various warrior tribes of pre-colonial Africa. In such a society the army is made up of all the fit men of the tribe.

In the Greek city states all free men were supposed to give military service at an appropriate age. Sparta, of course, was a famous example of a militarized society in which every free man was a soldier. Alexander the Great conquered the world with an army made up of a mixture of volunteers, conscripts and foreign mercenaries. In Rome men between 17 and 60 owed the State military service. As mentioned already, the only recorded objectors to this system were Christians.

After the fall of Rome and the dissolution of its empire defence became a local matter. The nobles in various parts of Europe fought the barbarians (and each other) in a piecemeal fashion with armies made up of cavalry and foot soldiers. The cavalry consisted of knights on heavy horses, a system adapted from Persian models. Persia had developed a heavy horse capable of standing in battle against the Mongols who rode light swift horses. Similarly, the European knight mounted on a heavy horse and clad in armour was able to withstand attack by swift lightly armed barbarians. These knights in armour were noblemen, that is, they belonged to a caste which had positive military obligations to serve personally and to raise corps by feudal levies.

An exception to this method of warfare grew up in Switzerland which is not suited to heavy cavalry or fighting in iron clothing. The Swiss developed militia of foot soldiers armed with pikes which were able to engage successfully with horsemen. Switzerland was thus the home of the earliest European citizen armies of conscripted but part-time and amateur soldiers used almost entirely for defensive purposes and rarely travelling outside the borders of the cantons. Sweden too had a citizen army which, however, was not always confined to defensive warfare.

Standing professional armies appeared in Europe in

about 1450 but did not become important until 1798. In the seventeenth century the developing nation states of Europe in the main had armies officered by noblemen – that is, men of the warrior caste, who led forces made up chiefly of unemployable riff-raff. The peasants and middle classes were exempt from military service. Their work was needed to keep society running and to provide equipment and food for the armies. Mercenaries sometimes supplemented the relatively small native forces. As well as standing armies there were militia forces of a more or less compulsory kind in Switzerland, Sweden, France, Spain and Prussia.

The eighteenth century saw the beginning of large conscripted non-defensive citizen armies officered by professionals who were not always nobles. France introduced conscription after the Revolution. The method used was compulsory registration and it eventually provided Napoleon with two million men over a period of 14 years.

A particularly horrible form of compulsion was impressment, or seizure. Cromwell used this method; so did the English Navy. In Russia until 1860 conscripts were impressed and served for life. In the 1870s Russia introduced universal military service: yet it allowed the Mennonite communities living within its borders to work in the forestry service as an alternative to entering the armed forces.

In the nineteenth and twentieth centuries compulsory military service became the rule all over continental Europe. Britain, though, did not introduce conscription until 1916, halfway through the First World War, abolishing it in 1919, and re-introducing it in the Second World War.

The USA introduced conscription in 1917, and again in the Second World War. It used compulsory registration followed by selective conscription to raise an army for the Vietnam War.

The oldest form of conscription is that used to train a local militia or citizen reserve for mainly defensive purposes. The Greeks and the Romans had militia forces. Anglo-

Saxon tribal law made every able-bodied free male liable for military service for local defensive purposes.

Modern compulsion usually takes the form of registration followed by a call-up of all or some of those registered.

Mercenaries may be volunteers, like the men who join the French Foreign Legion, or conscripts, like the Hessians sold to various nations and commanders by their princes in the eighteenth century.[2]

The refusal by Maximilianus of Numidia to give military service is one of the first recorded examples of explicit, personal, religious conscientious objection to engaging in war. It seems probable that other Christians were also put to death specifically on account of this form of non-co-operation during the more general persecutions. The conversion of the Emperor Constantine seems to have been followed by a considerable diminution of the anti-war traditions of the early Church, and the barbarians certainly did not do much to de-militarize Christianity. Yet even in the Dark Ages the connection between Christianity and the rejection of war did not entirely disappear; it survived in the rule that bloodshed, even in war, requires penance and absolution.

From the twelfth century onwards more robust forms of pacifism appeared which generally seem to have been based on the re-discovery, as it were, of the New Testament, and to have occurred amongst artisans, peasants, scholars and the lower clergy, that is, people not of the military caste.

The followers of Peter Waldo of Lyons (Waldensians), a sect which appeared in France in the twelfth century, held as one of their tenets a refusal to take human life in any circumstances. They were persecuted by the Inquisition, and in the fifteenth century they gave up pacifism and resisted their oppressors with armed force.

In Bohemia a New Testament-based sect, the Unity of Czech Brethren, did not allow its members to accept conscription into the armed forces.

In Zurich in the sixteenth century Konrad Grebel reintroduced adult baptism and is thus the founder of the *Anabaptists*, or *Re-Baptizers*. Grebel taught non-resistance and non-violence, and the Swiss Brethren held to the view that the rule 'resist not evil' is absolutely mandatory for believing Christians. Anabaptists were persecuted in Switzerland and elsewhere, but Anabaptist sects have survived, of course, and missionary activities, together with various emigrations, have taken them all over the world. In places, though, the association of adult baptism with pacifism disappeared rather quickly. In Poland, for example, after a visit by an Anabaptist missionary in the sixteenth century, some members of the nobility joined the sect: these professional soldiers and rulers were not prepared to give up the sword even in theory.

The experiences of conscientious objectors in Europe in the sixteenth and seventeenth centuries were different in different places. In Catholic countries members of pacifist sects were persecuted as heretics and tended therefore to lapse or to move elsewhere. Poland was a partial exception as the only Catholic country to accord official toleration to the Mennonites, the followers of Menno Simons, a Catholic priest who had converted to the doctrines of pacifism and adult baptism. In Protestant Switzerland young men were obliged to serve in the militias and conscientious objectors were not exempted. As a result the pacifist sects in Switzerland dwindled through lapsing and emigration. Emigration later became one of the standard responses of Mennonites, Quakers, and other pacifists to the introduction of conscription in European lands.[3]

According to Peter Brock the first important official recognition of conscientious objectors as a special category to be exempted from military service occurred in the Netherlands in the sixteenth century when William of Orange, faced with citizens who refused to serve in the army, allowed them to substitute other forms of service such as the payment of war taxes.

When communities of pacifist sects went into exile they were sometimes exempted from military service by their adoptive countries. For instance, during the reign of Maria

Theresa some communities of Hutterites, a branch of the Anabaptists, began to move around Europe because of her attempts to extirpate heresy. They spread into what is now Romania, and were eventually given permission by the Emperor of Russia to settle in his domains. Later Russia formally exempted them from military service.

During the nineteenth century universal conscription became the norm in Europe, and in general it ceased to be legally possible for a conscripted man to buy himself out by paying for a substitute. Clearly this solution had been of no use to poor men anyway; neither could it be thought of as really consistent with pacifist doctrines.

The rise of nationalism and of large nation states led to a withdrawing of any privileges or exemptions formerly enjoyed by sectarian conscientious objectors. Nationalism affected pacifist communities more directly too, in that their leaders sometimes successfully urged on them the idea that service in the army of a modern republic was quite different in kind from service in the armies of the *ancien regime*. Some German Mennonites fought in the Franco-Prussian War; and in 1934 the German Mennonites officially abandoned their adherence to pacifism, thus enabling themselves to take part in Hitler's wars. On the other hand the Mennonite communities of America have remained strictly anti-war-ist.[4]

The combination of civil war and sectarian theological strife seems to be a good recipe for generating pacifist ideas. Quakerism, founded by George Fox shortly after the end of the English Civil War, is an example, perhaps. A number of Fox's early followers had in fact been supporters of the victorious parliamentary party in the Civil War, though Fox himself had refused a commission in the Commonwealth army. In 1660 the Quakers adopted an explicitly pacifist (anti-war-ist) position; this enabled them to represent themselves to Charles II as 'harmless folk' of no danger to the State. They did not escape persecution, though, either then or later. But when William Penn obtained a grant of land in America from Charles, he was able to found the state of Pennsylvania as a place of refuge for Quakers, and as a model nation based on pacifist principles. Penn rejected the violence of war but accepted the necessity of the force of the magistrate, though he held that this force must be kept to a minimum. Pennsylvania dealt with the Indians on its borders according to what it described as its non-violent, just, and neighbourly principles, and either for this or for some other reason the province (according at least to Quaker authors) was for a long time free of the savage frontier warfare suffered by other American colonies.

Although Quakerism has followers in many lands it is in origin an Anglo-American sect and has its chief numerical strength in the English-speaking nations. In peace time these nations have usually raised their armies from volunteers, so it is only in time of war that Quaker citizens in America and the British Commonwealth are personally faced with the question of conscientious objection. But, as has already been noted, Quaker anti-war-ism goes far beyond personal conscientious objection.

The 1916 Military Service Act contained a 'conscience clause' which Quaker MPs and those of the Independent Labour Party had insisted on in parliament. Even so the Society of Friends opposed compulsory military service as such, as a matter of fundamental principle; and some members were gaoled for publishing and distributing anti-conscription pamphlets. The conscience clause of the 1916 Act allowed conscientious objectors to apply for exemption from bearing arms. Objectors had to appear before tribunals at which representatives of the armed forces appeared in the role of lawyers appealing against decisions which led to exemptions. Some exemptions were unconditional, others involved alternative service. It is notorious that some conscientious objectors were very badly treated, but it would seem that this was the fault of jingoes on the tribunals and in the army and not due to any special harshness in the Act itself. Public opinion was hostile to pacifism, which it perceived as treason or cowardice or both.

On the whole, American pacifists had a less difficult time

during the First World War than British pacifists. Members of well-known pacifist sects like the Mennonites had little difficulty in obtaining exemption from military service. In Britain pacifists were treated more humanely in the Second World War than in the First.

Although conscription as such is abhorrent to pacifists, it is clear that some forms of conscription are otherwise much worse than others. For instance, to be compelled to undertake part-time military training in an army designed for purely defensive purposes and stationed always in the homeland is very different from being conscripted for service abroad, in colonies, say. Serving abroad for one's own country is not as bad as being sold as an unwilling mercenary to a foreign state. Nothing could be much worse than being impressed for life: this type of conscription is no better than slavery.

Can one be a conscientious objector in the nuclear age? There are difficulties. According to some estimates an all-out nuclear war will last for seven minutes; other estimates say that such a war might last for six or seven days. War-time conscription is therefore impossible. Secondly, nuclear war does not need large armies, only a core of trained personnel to man missile bases and submarines. At present the USA and UK have no need to conscript people to man bases and submarines; financial inducements are enough. Thirdly, it would perhaps not be feasible to conscript men for nuclear war because unwilling men might refuse to press the button.

Where and when can a conscientious objector object, then? Plainly only before a nuclear war starts. And if there is no conscription his objection cannot take the form of a personal refusal to go into the army. It will have to take the form of a decision not to take part in any preparations for war. Such preparations are no longer merely military; they include for example all kinds of scientific work directed at the invention of weapons and delivery systems. The development of these systems and weapons has become extraordinarily rapid, which must indicate that enormous resources of money and manpower are involved. Perhaps in some places there is no longer any other kind of work, or perhaps there is no other kind of work for trained people. Still, a man who won't join an army but who is willing to work as a scientist (say) in this sort of endeavour is not a pacifist.

4

Violence and Contradiction

The most radical possible theoretical objection to pacifism is the claim that its thesis is self-contradictory. However, for reasons that should soon become apparent, this objection will not make much sense – nor, naturally, will its refutation – unless we are clear what we are talking about when we use the word *violence*. It is necessary therefore to begin by explaining the idea of violence.

What is violence? The word has been re-defined by political polemicists of both right and left. The left stretch the meaning so that many activities which in themselves involve no physical force are said to be violent in a new, semi-technical sense; while the right subject the term to a kind of surgery the result of which is that only the illegal use of force can be called violence. It is natural for polemicists to seek terminological advantages over their opponents, and the stipulative re-definition of words which are important in political or ethical debate is one of the easiest ways of creating the appearance of advantage. Slogans and new coinages can also confer advantage of this kind. It isn't really possible to prove anything by changing the usages of words, but unfortunately you can convince people without proving anything.

Re-definition, sloganizing and new coinage tend to distort but don't distort invariably. A slogan can give a needed name to an idea (e.g., 'male chauvinism'), or draw attention to unnoticed historical facts (as with 'property is theft'). A new coinage can serve as a mnemonic for a whole bookful of reasoning – think of the word *species-ism*, for example.[1] Still, whether the facts are salient, whether the idea is a good one, and whether the reasoning is sound are all of them further questions.

I shall now briefly examine some proposed ways of looking at violence. These are embodied in the terms 'structural violence' and 'institutional violence'. The second of these is or could be a useful expression but the first, 'structural violence', is bound to cause confusion.[2]

Structural violence is a name for what would more correctly be called *social injustice*. Sometimes it is even used to refer to ordinary personal injustice. Structural violence is said to be exemplified by laws or entrenched customs which restrict the choices available to some group or groups within a community – as it might be, blacks, or women, or members of a low caste – by fostering or creating invidious inequalities of opportunity, income, education or esteem. It does not of itself consist in or necessarily involve physical force. For although injustice, like justice, may often need to be secured or shored up by the threat or use of force, that is not invariably so. Because of this, structural violence is sometimes called *quiet violence* – non-violent violence, as it were.

Why would any one prefer to describe sets of unfair laws (say) as violent rather than as unjust? I think there are three reasons. If someone advocates revolution or terrorism he wants to be able to counter the accusation of violence with the counter-accusation 'and you are too!' This is a simple kind of justification, much used in fact by small boys, but grownup men find its words strangely powerful when uttered by themselves. Secondly, the change from talking about justice to talking about violence creates an implicit appeal to the right of self-defence. The right to defend oneself against direct attacks which threaten the physical integrity of one's person is acknowledged by every theory of rights (as far as I know). Most people, including even some pacifists, believe, too, that this right of self-defence against bodily attack includes a right to use at least some physical force in at least some circumstances. Now direct physical attack is a paradigm of violent behaviour. Violence, then, entails a correlative right to self-defence which may rightly take the form of counter-violence. But other forms of wrong (unfairness, deceit, etc.) do not obviously entail a right to hit back physically. It may be that I ought to put up with those kinds of wrong, when my physical integrity is not threatened, rather than damage another person's body. The right to fight injustice does not seem to automatically include a right to use physical force. By giving social injustice the new name 'structural violence' the polemicist at once makes it appear as if the right to self-defence can be appealed to, and with it the right to use some degree of countervailing physical force, or violence in the ordinary sense of the word. Thirdly, some theorizers have a strong tendency to look for simple unitary explanations of things. To some individuals a moral system which rests on more than one fundamental concept (as it might be, on fairness *and* truthfulness *and* non-violence) seems untidy. It looks possible to cut through a lot of difficulties if you can reduce all wickedness to just one type, for then there is no need to decide whether equality is better than liberty (say), or whether it is morally better to tell lies than to forgo the dole (for example). All actions will turn out to be good or bad according to whether or not they are 'violent'; and if 'violent', then to what degree. 'Structural violence' is semi-permanent, so it is judged to be worse than the allegedly temporary violence of revolution or terrorism.

Institutional violence would be a useful term if it could be clearly distinguished from *structural violence*. *Institutional violence* means, or could mean, legal violence, including the violence of legal institutions such as the police and the hangman. There is indeed such a thing as the violence of legal institutions (it might even be necessary for civilization). To use the expression *institutional violence* in this way might immunize debates about violence against a kind of terminological advantage sometimes seized by polemicists of the right, in whose work the word *violence*, having undergone surgery, is used to refer only to the *illegal* use of physical force. Institutional or legal violence can be thought of as having two varieties. There is the kind of physical violence against persons which occurs when police authorities enforce the provisions of the law, when prison warders control prison riots, and so on; and there is the use of physical force against persons which is carried out by ordinary citizens with the permission or with the encouragement of the law: for example, corporal punishment of children, sport (boxing), citizen's arrests, etc. In the real world social arrangements (just or unjust) usually need to be upheld by some near or distant threat of physical force. If the social arrangements are grossly unfair much actual force may be needed. For instance the social injustice ('structural violence') of apartheid naturally leads to a lot of institutional violence in the form of police action. So in a way it is easy to confuse the institutional with the structural: the confusion is partly one between cause and effect.

What is violence really, then? Primarily it is the use of physical force to injure, harm or constrain someone. Violent actions are those liable to cause bodily injury; to do violence to someone, to lay violent hands on someone, is to harm him physically or try to harm him; to die a violent death is to die as the result of injuries inflicted by an agent or sustained in an accident. There are also metaphorical uses which mostly mean *strong, forceful, severe, vehement, noisy, rapid* and the like. Thus the actions of the winds and the waves and other natural forces can be violent, colours may clash violently, and it is possible to be swayed by violent emotions, to speak violently, to suffer from violent headaches, fevers or fits, and even to give violent snorts of disgust. Last but not least it is possible to do violence to language by misusing words. The polemicist's re-definition of violence makes use of the conceptual connection with the idea of injury: 'structural violence' is whatever causes or helps cause or fails to prevent a significant social injury or harm.

If pacifism were a self-contradictory doctrine there would not be much point in subjecting it to any further examination. Well, is it possible to show that the thesis of pacifism contains a formal defect? One writer, Jan Narveson, has tried to demonstrate that pacifism is (as he variously puts it) 'incoherent', 'morally inconsistent' and 'self-contradictory in its fundamental intention'. As he is the sole defender of this position (as far as I know) it may be worthwhile to examine his arguments.[3]

Narveson insists that his proof is 'logical' not 'empirical', that is, that it does not depend on facts about how the world is. On the other hand he occasionally flits across a logical gap or weakness by using the phrase 'other things being equal'. But since he does not say which other things are relevant, nor, *ergo*, in what way they may be equal or unequal, I shall ignore this qualification as empty. Secondly, it should be noted that Narveson throughout his paper uses the words *violence* and *force* interchangably; yet at one point (pp. 72–3) he implies that *force* only means anything (including magic speech acts) that will get someone to do something against his own inclination. If that were what *force* meant, then force could not be equated with violence, nor would it be what any pacifist, conditional or unconditional, is against. The defensive use of means of a kind which cause no injury has never been regarded as evil even by the most absolute of absolute pacifists. Narveson's argument will not be relevant to pacifism if under *force* and *violence* he means to include the use of non-injurious actions (such as hypnotism) in defensive situations. So I shall interpret his argument as being about violence, that is, about uses of physical force which are actually, or at the very least potentially, injurious – violence in the ordinary sense of the word.

Narveson's argument has several steps, which I have numbered for ease of reference. In what follows I have often used his own words.

Definition: Pacifism is the principle that the use of violence to meet violence is wrong as such, that is, nobody may do so without special justification. This means that nobody has a right to fight back when attacked, that fighting back is inherently evil . . . (and) that we are all mistaken in supposing we have a right of self-protection . . . we have no right to punish criminals . . . all our machinery of criminal justice is . . . unjust.

(1) To say that something is morally wrong is to say that those to whom it is done have a moral right not to have it done to them.

(2) A right just *is* a status justifying preventive action: the denial of this is self-contradictory. To say that a man ought not engage in violence is to say precisely the same thing as that violence may justifiably be used to prevent his using violence.

(3) It follows logically from (2) that one has a right to do whatever may be necessary to prevent infringements of one's right.

(4) It is a logical truth that what might be necessary to prevent the infringement of one's right is the use of force (violence).

(5) (Initial conclusion): If we have any rights at all we have a right to use force to prevent the deprivation of the thing to which we have a right.

(6) The amount of force (violence) needed will be whatever amount is enough to prevent the infringement of the right. What is enough will depend on circumstances, including whether or not there exist laws, police, courts, etc.

Conclusion: the thesis of pacifism is the denial of (5): pacifism therefore is self-contradictory.

Narveson's definition of pacifism is defective, since there are several varieties of pacifism. He excuses his narrow definition by saying that it describes 'the most philosophically interesting' version of pacifism. He does not explain why he thinks a (supposedly) self-contradictory thesis is philosophically interesting. Furthermore, in spite of his acknowledging that he is talking only about some rather extreme variety of pacifism, at the end of his paper he jumps to the conclusion that everything that he has said applies automatically to other kinds of pacifist as well. Thus, he refers there explicitly to Vietnam war resisters: now *those* pacifists did not reject the right of self-defence; they are best described as *just war pacifists*. His proof, even if it succeeded, would not apply to these people, nor would it apply to Quakers and others who accept the State's right to use force against criminals.

To be self-contradictory a thesis or doctrine must *contain* a contradiction: it is not enough for it merely to contradict some other thesis or premise, for example, some premise about rights. The thesis of pacifism, even on Narveson's definition, does not as such include (1) the proposition that everything which is morally wrong is a violation of a right, nor (2) the thesis that a right just *is* a status justifying preventive action, nor (3) the thesis that one has a right to whatever may be necessary to prevent infringements of one's rights. Even if it contradicted these premises that would not make it *self*-contradictory.

Still, everyone must accept as true those propositions which are logically necessary or tautological. Now, perhaps some of Narveson's premises are tautological; or perhaps his initial conclusion (5) is tautological. And perhaps the thesis of pacifism contradicts one of these premises, or contradicts this initial conclusion: in which case it will itself be self-contradictory or logically false.

Consider premise (1). Is it a logically necessary truth that if a type of action is morally wrong then those to whom it is done have a right not to have it done to them? In other words, does every moral wrong have a correlative moral right which it violates? This seems unlikely because not every morally wrong action or type of action involves injury to an identifiable person or group of persons. Consider, for example, the well-known vices of boasting, snobbery, greed, cowardice and lying. These are all regarded as morally obnoxious, i.e. wrong. Yet boasting violates no rights. Snobbery may well cause pain but in general it does not violate rights except when it combines with other wrongs, for instance with an injustice, or with the kinds of deeds which flow from an indolent disregard for the needs of unimportant people. Ordinary greed for food and drink violates no rights except in situations of shortage (which may indeed be endemic at the world level). Greed for friends, fame, attention, may cause various kinds of rather disgusting behaviour, but behaviour which is rather disgusting does not necessarily violate any rights. Cowardice, unless excused by mental or physical illness, is widely regarded as morally contemptible, i.e., wrong, yet it only violates right in certain contexts; this is because it is possible to act in a cowardly way even when alone on a desert island.

Untruthfulness, in contrast to cowardice, greed and boasting, is a kind of wrong which in my view does inflict injury, though not necessarily physical injury. A lie is in itself an injury inflicted on the person who is lied to: everyone who is lied to and knows it feels this. Does it straight away follow that those who are lied to have a right not to be lied to? Is the inflicting of an injury on an identifiable person a necessary and sufficient condition for the violation of one of his rights? Injury *might* be a necessary condition but to regard it as a sufficient condition trivializes the whole concept of right. It empties the idea of most of its useful content if we insist that we have a right not to be snubbed, a right not to be gossiped about, a right not to have jokes made at our expense, a right not to be kept waiting by unpunctual friends, in other words a right not to be inconvenienced in any way by others. So even if injury were a necessary condition for violation of a right (which is doubtful), it is not a sufficient condition.

Although for these reasons it can be seen that premise (1) 'To say that something is morally wrong is to say that those to whom it is done have a moral right not to have it done to them' is false, a similar but weaker premise might be true. This is the premise:

> (1a) Those morally wrong actions which inflict *serious* injury on *identifiable individuals* are *ipso facto* violations of rights. Any serious violence unjustly inflicted on someone would be a violation of a right.

This is all that Narveson needs in the way of a premise at this point.

(2) Is it true that 'a right just *is* a status justifying preventive action'? Plainly the *is* here is not the *is* of identity, for infractions of rights are not the only things that justify preventive action; the threat of a smallpox epidemic also justifies preventive action, but I do not suppose many people would want to say that a right can be held against a bacillus. Then is the statement logically necessary though not an identity? Does the threatened violation of a right automatically justify preventive action? If this is true it is a truth heavily hedged about with *ceteris paribus* clauses for reasons that will appear shortly. And the more trivial the rights we allow the heavier the hedging.

Is it true that the proposition that a man ought not to engage in violence is 'precisely the same' proposition as the proposition that the use of violence to prevent him is justifiable? This alleged identity has no intuitive appeal and, needless to say, it is not recognized by the law. Furthermore, the formula of the complete statement does not guarantee truth. What I mean is, the substitution of names of other types of moral wrong for the word *violence* produces absurdities. Thus it is absurd to say that the proposition that a man ought not to engage in cheating is 'precisely the same' proposition as the proposition that the use of cheating is justifiable to prevent him doing so. Again it is obvious that the proposition that a man should not engage in bribery and corruption is by no means 'precisely the same' as the proposition that others may justifiably engage in bribery and corruption if that is the only way to prevent him. (It might be that these means of preventing cheating, bribery and so on would not be very effectual in the real world but that is not relevant in an argument which is meant to be non-empirical).

If for violence in general we try substituting in our premise or formula certain particular varieties of violence, the results which appear are even more unpleasant. Is the proposition that a man should not go in for torturing hostages 'precisely the same' proposition as the proposition that he may justifiably be tortured himself to prevent this? Is the proposition that a man ought not to engage in the slave trade 'precisely the same' proposition as the proposition that he may justifiably be sold into slavery to prevent this? What about nations? Is the proposition that a nation at war ought not to kill, starve or toture prisoners of war 'precisely the same' proposition as the proposition that in order to prevent this its own captured soldiers may justifiably be killed, starved and tortured?

The statements formed by substituting for violence in general particular kinds of violence or formed by substituting for the moral wrong of violence other types of moral wrong look like a childish kind of logic coupled with a very primitive moral code, a morality of savages. I see no reason, intuitive or other, to accept them as necessary truths or as statements of propositional identity, and no reason, either, for regarding the original premise (2) as a statement of genuine propositional identity. But if it is not a genuine identity it is false.

Premise (3) 'One has a right to whatever may be necessary to prevent infringements of one's right' is said to 'follow logically' from premise (2) 'A right just *is* a status justifying preventive action'. But it obviously *doesn't* follow: we might as well say that 'having a sore throat is a good reason for kidnapping a doctor' follows logically from 'being ill is a good reason for seeing a doctor'.

Well, is (3) true anyway, independently of (2)? It can't be true. For it is a logically necessary truth that 'whatever may be necessay' to prevent an infringement of a right *might* involve doing something that constitutes an even more serious violation of someone else's right. Accidental circumstances may determine whether or not that happens to be the case. This is a commonplace of moral philosophy in general and of rights theory in particular. Hence it cannot be true that one's right to prevent infringements of one's rights is open-ended in the way Narveson thinks it is. This also shows (incidentally) that if one tries to reduce all moral questions to questions of rights one ends up in various impasses that were not there when one began. (What's so special about rights, anyway?).

(4) This premise is true, i.e., it expresses a logical truth.

(5) 'If we have any rights at all we have a right to use violence to prevent infringement of those rights'. Does this initial or interim conclusion follow from premises (1) to (4)? And if not is it true anyway?

Premise (1), as we have seen, is false, though a weaker version of it might be true. Premise (2) is false. Premise (3) is also false, and it does not follow from premise (2). Even if the interim conclusion does follow from the premises the proof fails because of the falseness of the premises. However, is the interim conclusion true nevertheless, true independently of these premises?

It cannot be self-evidently true since it is logically possible for a violent defensive action to violate another's right, for example by being excessive, or by being a case of deliberately harming an innocent bystander (and thus violating *his* right). It cannot be true that if we have rights at all we have a right to violate the right of others in order to prevent the infringement of our own rights. That would reduce talk of rights to a nonsense. The corollary (6) is also not self-evidently true since the amount of violence needed to prevent an infringement of a right might easily turn out to involve worse harms and injuries than those of the original infringement of right. That is, the cure may be worse than the disease – even, in the long run, from the point of view of the individual whose rights were originally threatened. Further, just as not all harms involve violations of rights so, conversely, not all violations of rights necessarily involve harms. For instance if you and I have a contract and you break that contract then in doing so you violate my legal rights and also, *ceteris paribus*, my moral rights: but since your breach of contract automatically absolves me from any duty to perform my side of the bargain it could easily in some circumstances turn out to be to my benefit rather than to my harm. I conclude that there are many cases in which it is not reasonable to insist on one's rights, and many cases in which it is self-defeating to do so. Now it is not self-evident that 'if we have any rights at all' we have an absolute right to be absolutely unreasonable.

Then do we after all have no right to defend our rights? If rights are a serious matter then surely we do have a right to protect our rights. But this right cannot be open-ended. Some things may not be done in defence of rights. For example, seriously injuring the rights of others in ways that involve much worse harm than that threatened in the first place cannot be a permissible method of defending one's rights. There might sometimes be a duty to forgo a right. (This is part of the answer to the question: What's so special about rights anyway? Rights are not overridingly special and the theory of rights cannot by itself provide answers to *every* problem in moral philosophy.) Now whether violence, the injurious use of force, is or is not one of the methods permissible in defence of rights is (of course) the substantive question at issue.

Narveson's overall conclusion is that the thesis of pacifism is self-contradictory and his basis for this seems to be the supposition that the thesis of pacifism contradicts or is the contrary of (it is not clear which) the interim conclusion (5), 'If we have any rights at all we have a right to use violence to prevent infringement of those rights'. But unless (5) is logically necessary, which it is not, we cannot infer that its denial is self-contradictory.

Narveson also gives another reason for concluding that the thesis of pacifism is self-contradictory. This further reason does not mention rights. It is

(7) '(to say) that the use of violence is never justified to prevent initial violence being done to one logically implies that there is nothing wrong with the original violence'. Well, is there really a logical implication here?

The form of Narveson's statement (7) is: 'It is never right to perform acts of type V in order to prevent acts of type V' *logically implies* 'No acts of type V are wrong'.

This is counter-intuitive to an extreme degree, for surely

what is logically implied is the contrary conclusion. That is to say 'It is never right to perform acts of type V in order to prevent acts of type V' *logically implies* 'There are some acts of type V which are wrong (i.e., those which are referred to first in the antecedent of this inference)'.

Of course, if the thesis that violence is never justified *were* self-contradictory, it would materially imply any and every true or false proposition: but this does not seem to be Narveson's point here.

The thesis of pacifism, even if this is taken to be the thesis that violence is always wrong, has not been shown to be self-contradictory. Has it (here) been shown to be false though not logically false? It is *prima facie* unlikely that an analysis, even a correct analysis, of a narrow circle of three concepts (violence, rights and moral wrong) could by itself show that pacifism is false. However, there are other arguments against pacifism.

5

The Violence of the State

Several philosophers have argued that the external violence of the state is a kind of extension of its internal violence, an activity analogous to seizing and punishing murderers and burglars. For these thinkers war can be justified by reference to the same sort of considerations that explain why it is necessary to have arrangements for preventing crime and for incarcerating criminals. It seems, further, that if one rejects these reasons one must in theory also reject the state itself. For crime control is one of the main purposes of the state. Now if the external violence of the state (which includes war) is the same sort of thing as its internal violence ('the violence of the magistrate'), and if the things which make the second kind of violence necessary also make the first kind necessary, then it would seem that there is no way in which a line can be drawn between rejecting war and rejecting (say) police action. Hence the only reasons for adopting pacifism (*qua* anti-war-ism) must be pragmatic reasons, not reasons of principle. A *principled* pacifism must reject all violence and the state itself.

It is possible, though, that the similarity between the state's external violence and its internal violence has been, if not invented, then at least exaggerated. Let us now look at the arguments of some of those who have argued for the similarity between external and internal violence.

St Augustine justifies war by justifying punishment. Both punishment and war, he says, are all right provided they are pursued in a spirit of compassion and with the motive of helping and improving the persons being punished or fought. A just state punishes criminals and fights wars as a father punishes his child. Augustine saw (of course) that the death penalty, which he also defended, is not like parental punishment and will not fit the theory that just punishment is a compassionate activity, so he gave it a different and more prosaic justification: the death penalty is needed for the good of the community not the good of the criminal.[1] But if war is akin to punishment at all it is surely most like the death penalty; any intention to help and improve the enemy presumably only applies to the survivors, or to princes perhaps.

The learned canonist Alfonso Tostado wrote in *circa* 1430 'Just war is simply a mode of legal execution'.[2]

Vitorio says that, since St Paul says it is lawful for rulers to use arms against wrong-doers in the community, it must also be lawful to use arms against foreign enemies.[3] The Apostle Paul's actual words (as translated in the King James Bible) are: '. . . the powers that be are ordained of God. Whosoever therefore resisteth the power, resisteth the ordinance of God, and they that resist shall receive to themselves damnation. For rulers are not a terror to good works, but to the evil . . . if thou do that which is evil, be afraid, for he beareth not the sword in vain; for he is the minister of God, a revenger to execute wrath upon him that doeth evil'.[4] This is quite in line with the Jewish idea that God uses men (both good men and wicked men) to punish those whom he wishes to punish: that is, it is not inconsistent with the notion that rulers are wicked nor even with the notion that the work of ruling is evil work.

Calvin, too, thinks that war and punishment are much the same thing. He says, for example, that kiling soldiers in war is like exacting the death penalty on a criminal.[5]

Some more recent philosophers seem to have taken it as read that pacifism either *is*, or *ought (for the sake of consistency) to be*, an opposition to all violence, but especially the internal violence of the state. Thus G. E. M. Anscombe writes 'I take the doctrine of pacifism to be that it is *eo ipso* wrong to fight in wars', and then, two pages later, '. . . pacifist doctrine, i.e., condemnation of the use of force by the ruling authorities'.[6]

Now it is, I think, beyond question that very many pacifists, and particularly the Quakers, accept the necessity for the violence or threat of violence which secures the enforcing of laws. On the other hand, we should note that Quakers, and probably other pacifists as well, are opposed to the death penalty and in general think that the 'violence of the magistrate' should be reduced to a minimum.

Now, is there any inconsistency in accepting the need for whatever violence has to be used to enforce the law inside a state and at the same time holding that the violence of war is completely impermissible? There is only *inconsistency* if war on the one hand, and communal or state punishment on the other, are really one and the same thing. If they are different kinds of thing then what justifies the one will not *necessarily* justify the other. (The question as to whether either war or civil punishment is much like the punishment a father gives his children surely deserves a negative answer).

The fact that in St Paul's time and in St Augustine's time and for many centuries afterwards the two jobs of internal policing and external defence were generally carried out by the same organisation, namely the army, does not by itself show that the two tasks are the same. Barbers used also to be surgeons, but the two tasks are clearly different.

It can easily be argued that there are many differences between the use of civil force or violence inside a state, and warfare. Neither police action nor judicial process is much like military action, and punishment is not at all like war.

Anti-pacifists arguing that war is just like police action usually omit to mention that police action isn't always all right. Sometimes the actions of a police force are downright evil; this seems often to be the case in certain South and Central American Republics. Similarly the anti-pacifist move which runs 'If you reject the state's right to wage war you must also, to be consistent, reject its help in protecting you against robbers' fails to consider the possibility that any right you might have to call in the police must depend initially on how the police are likely to behave when you do call them in. It is only in fairly civilized countries that the citizen's moral right to call in the police can be taken for granted. If the police force is the Ton Ton Macoute it would not be right nor even sensible to ask for their help; if your local bobby is in the habit of behaving like certain military men – like the Crusaders in Jerusalem, or like the Black and Tans in Ireland, for example – it would not be wise or right to telephone him to report a missing bicycle.

In a civilized country punishment is in the first place a matter for the courts and subsequently a matter for the prison service. Even if there were to be an overlap of the personnel carrying out the jobs, it can still be seen that there are at least three different jobs here: there is the job of deciding on guilt, the job of deciding on the proper amount of punishment, and the job of carrying out the punishment once decided. The task of the police is a fourth: they are supposed to find and catch the criminal and bring him to the court. In civilized countries, for very good reasons, the police are not supposed to carry out the punishment of criminals; it would make crime detection too much like war. This rule also explains why it is actually humanly possible to insist that policemen should use a minimum of force when dealing with criminals. In warfare proper there is no parallel division of roles. If we insist on the alleged analogy we will have to allow that the battlefield is police beat, courtroom, gaol and execution block all rolled into one.

In some countries – admittedly only one or two – the police are unarmed, and perhaps in certain other countries police guns are less necessary than they are thought to be. Maybe they are sometimes carried for macho reasons. In civilized countries it is unusual rather than usual for a policeman to have killed people.

In a civilized country it is possible to sue the police. It is not possible for a vanquished nation to sue the victor.

In civilized countries policemen and judges and prison warders help in various ways to uphold laws to which they themselves are subject. When kings and generals and armies engage in warfare they are not upholding laws; certainly not laws to which they themselves are subject.

In even partly civilized countries the actions of the police and of the courts are more often effective than ineffective. It is assumed, one hopes rightly, that police activity will in the main help to protect lives and property and keep the peace and prevent riots and crime. A police force which is both active and ineffective is intolerable, a manifestation of tyranny. It cannot be seriously argued that warfare (especially modern warfare) protects lives and property. It cannot even be said that it is 'in the main effective', for war aims are rarely clear, they change as wars progress. Anyway it isn't obvious what counts as effectiveness in this context. Perhaps a war is effective for the winner in that he didn't turn out to be the loser, but the winner of a modern war does not effectively protect lives and property, even his own. He may lose more than he gains in property and of course all the lives lost are just completely and finally lost. As to moral effectiveness, there is no reason to suppose that the morally better side always wins or even wins more often than not.

Is war like judicial process? Is it like the punishment of criminals?

There can be no law which aims at the punishment of states. But it would be possible to have an international agreement that the inhabitants or the rulers or both of states vanquished in war should be punished. The inhabitants of Germany were punished by having to pay reparations after the First World War, though this was not decided on by anything resembling judicial process. Punishing inhabitants is not the same thing as punishing a state; nor could it be just, since inhabitants include infants, foreigners, and people opposed to war or to the war in question. And anyway only those living in vanquished states *could* be punished, whatever the justice of the cause.

In the trial, judgement and punishment of a criminal it is normally taken for granted that the judge and jury will not be themselves involved in crime. We would think it monstrous if judges and jurymen were themselves criminals, and doubly so if the crimes they were involved in were the very same ones as those of the man they were trying – if they were his rivals, say, or his accomplices. Such a state of affairs would constitute a terrible injustice and if common would be a manifestation of the worst kind of tyranny. In war each side may well claim to be punishing the other, yet it is quite common for both sides to be acting unjustly. There is no logical reason why both sides cannot act with tremendous injustice as to methods, and no logical reason why both sides cannot be unjust in their aims. For either the theory of the just war is a roughly adequate account of what a just war aim can be, or else there is no such thing as a just war at all. Now it follows from the theses of the traditional just war theory that the injustice of your enemy's war aim is a necessary but by no means a sufficient condition of the justice of your own war aim. And in fact it seems to be the case that in most wars both sides are unjust, at least to some extent, in their methods, and unjust, at least to some extent, in their aims.

In the preceding paragraphs some of the points made have been prefixed by the qualification 'in civilized countries.' This qualification does not affect the validity of my argument, the conclusion of which is not that the internal violence of the state might not physically resemble its external violence, but rather that the need for civil punishment cannot be a justification for war. The argument can now be put as a dilemma: if the arrangements for seizing, trying, sentencing and punishing criminals within the state are necessary, fair and non-tyrannical; in short, if they are reasonably civilized and functionally separate, then they will be too unlike warfare to justify that activity. If, on the other hand, those arrangements are of the kind made in countries run by tyrants and gangsters – where incidentally it is often likely to be the case that just one single organization (the army) carries out all the functionally separate tasks of the criminal law which are listed above – then they are not themselves justified and so cannot provide justification for anything else.

Latter-day just war theorists sometimes seem to feel forced to give new senses to the words *innocent*, *guilty*, and *unjust*. I shall say more about this matter in chapter seven, but for the moment it should be noted that in ordinary criminal law the objective injuriousness of an action is not a sufficient condition of its criminality. Guilt requires either intention or negligence, and sometimes other conditions as well. In warfare, according to some theorists, all combatants are guilty and all non-combatants are innocent. Conscription makes no difference since *guilt* means for these theorists in this context simply the fact of willingly or unwillingly carrying out an objectively injurious act. The distinction between guilt and innocence is preserved by changing the meanings of words. But how else can the theorist so much as use the terms *innocent* and *guilty*? In warfare most of the time most of the active participants do not know what is going on in the councils of state or even much of what goes on in the operations rooms of the generals: the only people who can count as guilty are the people who plan the war, not those who carry it out. And in fact this is what some just war theorists concluded: that soldiers as such are all normally innocent. But then what becomes of the dictum that the innocent must not be killed? Without re-definition of *guilt* and *innocence*, that thesis or the just war theory itself would have to be given up. In any case the re-definition seriously weakens any analogy between war and the civil punishment of criminals.

We might also note in passing that in the execution or other civil punishment of a criminal there is no real possibility of the executioner's having to worry himself about the famous principle of double effect, for there is no real possibility that he will indirectly or accidentally imprison, gas, electrocute or hang any of the criminal's relations or friends along with the criminal.

Lastly, it is possible for punishment to take many forms and it is no part of its essential nature that it should involve killing. It is empirically possible to abolish the death penalty. A state of affairs in which criminals (even desperate criminals) are never killed, either in the course of the attempts made to apprehend them, or subsequently as punishment, is logically possible. But war without death is logically impossible.

6

The Just War

The doctrine of the just war is the most important philosophical rejoinder to pacifism. It begins from the premise, discussed in chapter five, that the state's use of violence in war is similar to its exercise of force in internal jurisdiction. But since it follows from the theory itself that some wars are just, others unjust, it would seem that war can be like crime as well as like police work and punishment.

Pacifism *qua* anti-war-ism distinguishes between permissible and impermissible kinds of violence by drawing a line between the external and internal use of force by the state. The just war theory also draws a line between permissible and impermissible kinds of violence, but it draws it in a different place.

The traditional theory of the just war contains *inter alia* certain doctrines as to who may and who may not bear arms in war; otherwise its three main theses are as follows: a war to be just must be initiated and led by a proper authority, must be fought for a just cause with right intentions, and must not use illicit means.

The notion of a proper authority is inevitably ambiguous. In its perhaps primary sense of a rightful government or leader it ineluctably presupposes that satisfactory distinctions have already been drawn between different kinds of violence (for example, war, crime, capital punishment, and private vengeance), and between different kinds of groups (for example, gangs, guerrilla armies, villages, cities, and states). Thus *proper authority* has to be a classificatory term before it can be a legal or a moral one. Secondly, it may be worth noting that, in the tradtional theory, self-defence is by no means the only kind of just cause. In fact, the justice of self-defence is more or less taken for granted; it is the justice and injustice of aggression which receives most attention. Thirdly, it is also possibly worth noting that while the killing of innocent people is no doubt the main kind of injustice *in* war it is by no means the only one discussed by theorists in the past.

In what follows it is taken for granted that the questions raised by the theory of the just war are important as philosophy and not merely as history. Thus, the answers considered will sometimes be those given in the past and sometimes those we might consider rational today.

Who may or ought to fight in wars, and who ought not to?

Until the twentieth century women were everywhere exempt from military service in the civilized world. But in modern states the continually increasing mechanization of work has made a continually increasing percentage of citizens of both sexes available for military training and service. Even so, I think that many people still see the idea of women fighting in wars as abhorrent.

Should priests and other religious fight in wars? As has been noted already, the conversion of Constantine and the teachings of St Augustine dealt heavy blows at the early pacifist or quasi-pacifist aspects of Christianity. Nevertheless these aspects could not disappear entirely. One way of reconciling the teachings of Augustine with what can be read in the New Testament was to interpret the problematic passages in the Gospels as applying not to all men, and not even to all Christians, but only to 'those who would be perfect'. This expression in turn was interpreted as referring to priests and monks (and of course nuns) but not to lay people. Such interpretations, which can be found in, for example, Gratian and other earlier and later canonists,

were themselves dealt rather a blow by the ideology of the
Crusades. In any case, even before the Crusades, the clergy
did not always want to be exempted from fighting. Thus
we read in *The Song of Roland* a description of Archbishop
Turpin of Rheims first urging Charlemagne's lords and
barons into battle then joining in himself:

> My Lords, barons, Charles left us here for this;
> He is our king, well may we die for him:
> To Christendom good service offering.
> Battle you'll have, you are all bound to it,
> For with your eyes you see the Saracens.
> Pray for God's grace, confessing Him your sins!
> For your souls' health I'll absolution give;

Then when one of these barons is killed in action by a
Saracen:

> Swift through the field Turpin the Archbishop passed;
> Such shaven-crown has never else sung Mass
> Who with his limbs such prowess might compass;
> To th' pagan said "God send thee all that's bad!
> One hast thou slain for whom my heart is sad."
> So his good horse forth at his bidding ran,
> He's struck him then on his shield Toledan,
> Until he flings him dead on the green grass.

Once started, the good Archbishop did not stop:

> So Turpin strikes, spares him not anyway,
> After that blow he's worth no penny wage,
> The carcase he's sliced, rib from rib away,
> So flings him dead in an empty place.
> Then say the Franks "He has great vassalage,
> With the Archbishop surely the Cross is safe."[1]

Another priest, Bishop Odo of Bayeux, a brother of the
Conqueror, fought at the Battle of Hastings, where
according to legend he carried a mace instead of a sword so

that he could kill people without shedding their blood. (If Roman soldiers had carried maces instead of swords, St Peter would no doubt have been warned that 'he who lives by the mace shall die by the mace'.)

Gratian, though, writing in *circa* 1140, says that canon law forbids the clergy to fight. Other canonists of the twelfth and thirteenth centuries also take this view. It is usual for these writers to specify that a soldier cannot be a cleric. A few say that it is all right for clergy to carry arms, but only for the purpose of frightening enemies. On the other hand, some canonists state that wars against enemies of God – pagans, heretics and infidels – are an exception to the rule; and indeed clergy accompanying the Crusades did wear armour and carry swords.[2]

The view that clergy must not fight prevailed in the end, but the idea that it is only the clergy who can or should 'seek to attain perfection' by leading lives of non-violence has been challenged by Christian pacifists. The Quakers, for instance, could not possibly limit the seeking of perfection in this way to the clergy since they have no professional preachers and make no distinction between the lay and the religious.

Should the men of a subject race be conscripted to serve in the army of a conqueror or a colonial power? Such a state of affairs seems manifestly unjust, especially if men so conscripted are ordered under military discipline to fire on their own countrymen.

Who may or ought to initiate war? Is this a special role? If so, who holds it? The traditional answer, based on Aquinas, is that a war to be just must be initiated and led by a proper authority. But what is a proper authority? Well, there must be at least two ways in which someone can fail to be a proper authority. He might be, as it were, an improper authority, one who exercises political or princely power without having any right to do that. Or he might not be a ruler at all, not even a *de facto* one, but only a private citizen.

Those who, in fact, seize power by violence or guile are these days often generals, colonels, and the like; so that, being military men, they are in one sense well-fitted for waging war. Now, are all the wars waged by usurpers and revolutionaries necessarily unjust? This is not a feasible view for a just war theorist to hold, since if the wars waged by usurpers are unjust so too must those waged by the heirs of usurpers. But then there would hardly be any just wars; certainly very few in Europe. Either there are very few proper authorities and so very few just wars, or else proper authority is compatible with usurpation and revolution: proper authority in short is nothing less mundane than a matter of public international recognition. Still, the usurper's first war, his revolution or war of usurpation, is a different matter, for usually it will involve the overturning of a proper (recognized) authority. If the traditional rule of just war theory is correct, most revolutions and wars of usurpation are unjust and most instigations of revolution and usurpation are unjust.

The second way in which someone can fail to be a proper authority is by not being an authority at all. Aquinas's view is that it does not pertain to the private individual to make war; it is not his work, not his job. This raises questions about the classification of different types of violence to which just war theorists no less than pacifists need to find answers. Problems about classification are well illustrated in history and in our own day. For example, during the ninth and tenth centuries in Northern Europe the relationships between the political and quasi-political units which had inherited power from the Roman Empire and from Charlemagne were in practice very uncertain; furthermore, there was no universally accepted theory as to what those relationships ought to be. The lands occupied by the Franks were beset by 'wars' between small political units (such as cities, local lords, dependent princes), and the military caste, permanently ready for fighting of one kind or another, engaged in vengeful feuding and in looting church property and stealing from the peasantry. Canonists listing the decrees of popes and councils, and commenting on these, and on the inherited Code of Justinian, and on Augustine's discussions of war and violence, must naturally have been profoundly interested, for practical no less than for theoretical reasons, in questions about both the classification and the legality of various kinds of violence. It seems likely that their anxieties influenced the development of the theory of the just war.

The Council of Charroux held in 990 AD anathematized all those who robbed churches, stole beasts from peasants, or attacked unarmed clerks. Other local councils of the Church issued similar decrees between 975 AD and 1025 AD, excommunicating violent men, praying for peace and displaying relics of saints. The knights were told that ergotism, a disease prevalent at the time because of damage to rye crops caused by floods, was a divine punishment for violence and could only be cured by penances, fasting and veneration of certain relics. This attempt by the Church to curb civil violence was called *The Peace of God*. About 100 years later came the *Truce of God*, a movement which tried to outlaw fighting on certain days and at certain times (such as on Sundays and during Lent). In the eleventh century, too, the Council of Narbonne decreed that 'no Christian should kill another Christian: whoever does so sheds the blood of Christ'. This in effect was a demand for complete internal peace within Christendom; that is, the kind of internal peace that we nowadays expect to find enforced by law and custom and the police inside the borders of a civilized state. Certain powerful dukes who supported the Peace and the Truce enforced within their own territories the councils' bans on feuding. Gradually a new hierarchy of responsibility for internal jurisdiction began to develop, replacing that which had been lost after the breakup of the Carolingian Empire.[3]

The process of promoting internal peace was possibly helped by the actions of Urban II. Urban visited France in 1095 AD, calling upon Christian men to stop warring with each other and instead to dedicate their arms to the recapture of the Holy Land. The pope thus showed to the knights an external enemy whom they could attack with the sanction of the Church, or the sanction of Rome. This discovery of an external enemy a long way away must have removed many fairly lawless military men from Europe.

In our own time, bands of hijackers, guerrilla fighters, terrorists, etc., engage in armed violence directed sometimes against an identifiable enemy and sometimes against the nationals of countries not involved in the political issues which motivate the violence. Are these forms of violence warfare or crime or both? Are those who plan and carry out these deeds private individuals, or soldiers and governments-in-exile? Or are they would-be usurping powers?

A paradigm war is an armed conflict directed against an external enemy. But external to what? The notion of an external enemy presupposes the notion of an established political unit of some sort with a territory of its own. This, though, is only a necessary and not a sufficient condition for distinguishing between external and internal enemies. Independence is also needed, but how is that measured? The measure may often be simply pragmatic. A city council for example, though not a private person, cannot wage war, and its conflicts with other city councils or with county councils or the government count as internal, not external, conflicts. In the Dark Ages a baron in his stronghold was a kind of political unit, but whether his proper activities were supposed to be war or policing or private fighting was not exactly clear, to him or to anyone else. Our contemporary understanding of what counts as external conflict and what as internal rests largely on sheer facts, perhaps usually unnoticed facts. For example, there is the fact that for a long time most large-scale armed conflicts have been carried out by nation states. But what counts as a state, what counts as an external enemy, and what counts as a war are questions which all go together so that any brief answers will yield circular sets of definitions. The questions as to who or what is an authority logically capable of initiating and waging a just war rests ultimately both on facts about inherited customs and institutions (such as the Salic Law, the Constitutions of Clarendon, and the American Constitution), and on facts about *Realpolitik* (such as the actions of Palmerston, of Robespierre, and of Lenin); for it is these things that determine the identities of rulers and the boundaries of political units.

According to the traditional theory of the just war, it does not pertain to a private individual to wage war. This looks more like a dictum about what is lawful or right than like a classificatory rule. It suggests that private persons *can* wage war but only unjustly, illegally and without right. Is this true? Paradigm wars are initiated by *de facto* or constitutional rulers of political units of a kind which in their historical settings are or can be regarded as independent of other similar or larger units; they are led and directed by those rulers or by their agents; fought against enemies who are perceived as subjects or agents of a different state, and involve armed conflict on a relatively large scale. Nevertheless, in the end, sheer scale is of over-riding importance. If a multi-millionaire were to get together a large roving army of mercenary fighting men for the purpose of forwarding his own private business deals in various countries, then whether or not their activities were regarded as warfare or merely as piracy and banditry would, I believe, depend mainly on the scale of those activities as compared to the scale of other contemporary armed conflicts involving a lot of killing. In other words, large-scale piracy and banditry are species of warfare and, *ceteris paribus*, unjust warfare.

What kinds of violence are lawful or even good? In the tenth and eleventh centuries the clergy still allotted penances for killing human beings, and soldiers killing in battles were not exempted from these. H. E. J. Cowdrey, commenting on a number of tenth- and eleventh-century penitential texts and canons relating to killing (including a French penitential of 924 AD and the *Decretum* or collection of canon law made by Burchard of Worms in 1012 AD) writes '. . . all these sources are evidence for the continuance of the age-old view . . . that engaging in warfare, even at the command of a prince and in a just cause involves grave sin'.[4] Cowdrey describes an English penitential of Bishop Ermenfried, a papal legate to England in 1070, who confirmed a list of penances drawn up, probably in 1067, by

Norman bishops, and relating to the killings at the Battle of
Hastings. The penances laid down varied according to
motives, numbers of killings, and times of killings (for
example, whether they took place in the battle or after it).
For instance, those who fought and killed for personal gain
were supposed to do penance for seven years, whereas those
who fought and killed at the command of their prince
(Duke William) were only given three years. Penances
could be commuted by alms-giving, and according to
Cowdrey the building of Battle Abbey may have been
William's personal commutation of penances for the 2000
men he claimed to have personally killed at Hastings.

On the other hand, Pope Leo IV (847–55) had already
decreed that killing infidels was no murder. Leo promised
the Kingdom of Heaven (to which, of course, he officially
held the keys) to all those who died in wars against infidels.
Pope Urban II (1088–99) decreed that those who publicly
or privately killed excommunicated people were not guilty
of murder[5] and when he launched the First Crusade he said
that killing an infidel was not a sin.

Gratian, who in 1140 made a comprehensive collection of
Church canons, including the decrees of Leo IV, of Urban
II, and of the other popes between 560 and 1140, and
whose commentaries on these were influenced by his
reading of St Augustine, says that military service is not a
sin provided it is not done for gain or plunder. Military
action should only be carried out in the service of a
legitimate authority such as a prince, and it needs episcopal
permission. New Testament precepts of patience and non-
violence have to do with inner attitudes, not external
actions. Gratian compares war with judicial process and
punishment; now no penalty is incurred by proper authorities carrying out their proper tasks nor by those who
obey them and help them. Coercion of heretics and
Crusades against infidels are amongst the proper tasks of
Christian princes, as is evident, says Gratian, from various
papal decrees.

In the thirteenth century three kinds of licit violence
were distinguished by Pope Innocent IV. These are, first,

simple self-defence, which is a natural right and therefore needs no authority; second, the exercise of jurisdiction over subjects by a prince, which might involve battles but nevertheless is not the same thing as war; third, violence waged against an external enemy by an independent prince: this last is war and, according to Innocent, just war.[6]

What reasons for going to war are sufficient to justify the action? The traditional reasons include self-defence, the defence of the homeland, the defence of allies, the bringing about of a return to the *status quo* after theft of goods or expropriation of territory, the punishment of guilty persons (for example, 'warmongers', generals, war criminals, etc.), and the coercion of wrong-thinking people (as, for instance, heretics, infidels, etc). These traditional justifications for going to war are found (some here, some there) in Augustine's defence of war, in Justinian's laws, in decrees of popes and councils, in the writings of medieval commentators on those decrees, and in the works of theologians and philosophers both before and after Thomas Aquinas. Modern rulers still appeal to some more or less elastic version of one or other of the traditional grounds. Self-defence is the rationale of the two great military alliances, NATO and the Warsaw Pact; return of stolen land was the reason (on both sides) for the Falklands War; the desire to punish terrorists might well spark off at least a small war one day. If, *contra* pacifist thinking, war is ever justified, then the sufficient reasons for engaging in it must surely be found somewhere here.

What constitutes justice and injustice *in* war? What methods of war are evil, and what methods are all right? The question covers many different matters: truces, deceptions, kinds of weapons, treatment of prisoners, and of allies, and of innocent or non-combatant people.

Hobbes says that the keeping of truces, of promises once made, is a fundamental natural (moral) law.[7] Unless truces and promises can be relied on, no protagonist will surrender, every battle will be a fight to the death, and mankind will remain in a state of perpetual war. This idea has perhaps always been part of human thought; the Greeks, for instance, made truces in order to allow each side to bury its dead. The Romans also made truces with surrendering cities, who could only ensure the terms of a truce by appealing to Roman *fides*; it is said that such appeals were normally successful. Cities which refused to surrender, on the other hand, would be taken by storm.

Greek and Roman customs allowed the killing of captives and their enslavement. Looting and plunder were also allowed. Heralds, unlike prisoners, were supposed to be protected and given safe conduct. Temples were supposed to be sancrosanct. Surprise attacks were supposed not to be allowed, and generally speaking in those times people did not fight at night.

The rules of war given by Jahweh to the children of Israel, as reported in Deuteronomy 20, enjoined on them the extermination of the inhabitants of the land which he had promised to his Chosen People. Otherwise he ordered that, when enemies who refused to surrender were conquered, the men were to be killed and the women and children spared: enemies who surrendered were all to be spared but made to pay tribute.

On deception in war, Aquinas argues that ambushes, though deceptive, are not lies nor breaches of faith, and are therefore all right. He also says that fighting on feast days is allowable, citing the Book of Maccabees.

Aquinas argues that the killing of the innocent is always illicit, but does not seem to suppose that the proposition is self-evident, even to non-corrupt minds, for he gives four reasons in its support. First, killing the innocent harms those whom one ought to love out of charity; second, it harms those who deserve no harm; third, it deprives a community of something good, since innocent men are just men; fourth, it shows contempt for God.[8]

Feudal theologians allowed plunder and looting in a war being fought for a just cause. Albertus Magnus, in fact, recommended that foot soldiers should be given low wages, for then the prospect of plunder would make them fight bravely. But cavalry, he said, ought to fight bravely for the sake of honour.[9] Other writers, though, cite John the Baptist's advice to soldiers ('be content with your pay') as proof that looting is not lawful.

According to Roman law, captives in war could be enslaved by their captors, and feudal practice allowed prisoners to be held for ransom. Feudal theory was that non-Christians could be enslaved, but Christians could not.

The Spanish jurist Alfonso Tostado (born in 1400) says 'In a just war there is nothing that may not be wrought against the enemy except for a violation of the truth'.[10]

Francisco Vitorio (1480–1545) begins his second treatise on the law of war with a reference to those passages in the New Testament which appear to forbid self-defence – chapters five and 26 of St Matthew's Gospel, for instance. Like Augustine, he is at first puzzled as to how to get around these passages. He solves the problem by arguing 'from the reason of the thing'. The proof that war can be licit 'from the reason of the thing' is itself adapted from Augustine's analogical argument which asserts a similarity between the violence of internal jurisdiction and the violence of warfare.[11]

Vitorio's discussion of methods starts from the thesis that, the aim of war being the preservation of the state, everything which is necessary to that aim is permissible. This thesis, though, comes into conflict with another premise used by Vitorio, namely, the one which is drawn from the analogy of 'the reason of the thing'. That premise (implicit in much of what he says about the killing of the innocent) is that actions which would be illicit if carried out in the course of the proper exercise of internal jurisdiction are also illicit in war. The conflict between these two propositions leads him to lay down humane and reasonable rules which he then qualifies until they disappear. He has difficulties with the notion of innocence in war, and his account of what such innocence amounts to generates the conclusion that in many, perhaps in most wars, virtually every military participant and virtually every ruler and prince is innocent. For he says that a prince who starts an unjust war is innocent of injustice provided only that after pondering the matter carefully and consulting wise men he comes to *believe* – albeit wrongly – that his cause is just. As for the subject, unless he has access to the councils of state he has no obligation to enquire into the justice of the reasons for a war; his duty is to obey his prince. That a cause is judged just by the public authorities is all that ordinary men need to know. And again Vitorio appeals to 'the reason of the thing', for, he says, if a ruler had to explain the motives for a war to all the soldiers who were to fight in it, and moreover had to convince them of its justice, war would become impossible. The result of his theory about innocenece appears to be that soldiers are innocent whatever they do provided they act on the authority of their ruler. Thus they may loot and burn cities, kill prisoners, and so on, on the authority of a prince. Towards the end of his treatise on the laws of war, Vitorio's distinction between guilty and innocent has almost collapsed, but he does not seem to notice this. For instance, he begins by saying that it is always wrong to deliberately target and kill the innocent even in the heat of battle, and he gives, as examples of the innocent, children ('even of Turks'), 'harmless agricultural folk' and women. But he ends by explaining that although it is all right to kill soldiers in battle, it won't do to kill military captives *giving as his reason* the (putative) fact the *most soldiers are innocent.*

Vitorio urges restraint in warfare, even against infidels and pagans, but places no absolute ban on the use of weapons and methods which are likely to kill women and children, such as cannons, or the burning of walled cities. Neither does he place an absolute ban on the taking of hostages; nor on the killing of guilty hostages; nor on looting and plunder; nor on exacting reparations from conquered enemies. Such methods of waging war are wrong only relatively – that is, in cases where they exceed what is necessary to achieve victory. There are, as it were, *prima facie* reasons against the use of some weapons and some methods, but all such reasons are defeasible in the face of judgements of expediency, judgements of what is needed to win.

Grotius (1583–1645), in his work on war and peace,[12] distinguishes five kinds of law: divine law, natural law, civil law, the law of nations or international law, and canon law or the law of the Church. The law of nations is mainly concerned with war and peace. Grotius remarks that not all law is written law. This is especially true of international law; yet not all civil law is written either: much rests on precedent and custom, or simply on what men think ought to happen. He gives as an example the unwritten laws and customs relating to the burial or cremation of the dead. All nations respect each other's laws about the disposal of the dead and allow even their enemies to bury their dead after a battle. Not all law is backed by sanctions, but, says Grotius, law without sanctions is not entirely devoid of effects since men prefer to have a good conscience, they often respect justice and fear God, and a belief in the rightness of a cause makes soldiers fight bravely, whereas a belief that the cause is unjust makes them unwilling to fight at all. Those who think that all law has to be backed by sanctions and who argue consequently that there is no such thing as the law of nations forget about the existence of military and trade alliances. Power does not destroy the need for justice, though perfect justice would remove the need for power and courage.

Like earlier authors, Grotius says that the only good reason for starting a war is the righting of wrongs, and he also lists a number of common bad reasons for war. Thus he says that war started for pure love of fighting is the war of savages, while war started for persuasive but not justifying reason is the war of robbers. Other bad reasons are 'the fear of what is uncertain', for instance fear of a neighbour's possible future intentions as manifested by his exercise of the right to build defensive walls around his city; the discovery of a new land already inhabited by another people; a desire to rule others on the pretext that it would be for their own good; and rebellion by a subject nation. Even if a nation has been wronged and therefore has a right to wage war, it should, whenever possible, give up the right and try to settle matters by arbitration or conference or by

casting lots. For even just war is bad. Peace is more
important than freedom because the slaughter of a people is
the worst possible evil. Given the choice, it is better to
become slaves, as the Jews became slaves of the Baby-
lonians, rather than engage in a war of annihilation. The
ship is saved by casting out the cargo (liberty), not the
passengers.

What is permissible in war? Grotius distinguishes two
senses of *permissible*: that which can be done with impunity,
and that which can be done without injustice or wrong.

Whatever can be done with impunity will in fact be done,
he says, and furthermore whatever can be done with
impunity can (in a way) be properly described as a right of
war. The law of war is what nations customarily do in war
and what victors do with impunity. It includes (or allows):
killing the innocent (children, women, clerics and unarmed
folk generally); killing foreigners living in the enemy's
territory; killing or torturing prisoners of war and hostages
and spies; killing those who offer surrender terms and those
who surrender unconditionally; enslaving captives and all
their descendants born in captivity; killing or torturing
slaves; and the complete destruction of the enemy's state.
All victors, just or unjust, can do these things with
impunity, and therefore all victors have the right to do
them according to the law of nations or the law of war.
Grotius does, however, suggest that breaking faith in the
matter of treaties and agreed truces is not a right of war;
nor is rape 'among the better nations'; nor is the poisoning
of weapons, water or food. Yet surely if it is impunity that
confers the rights of war, he has no reason to exclude bad
faith, rape and poisoning. I think that his remarks at this
point are probably due to a slip or lapse, for one of his main
intentions is, precisely, to distinguish between a right in the
sense of what one can get away with, and a right in the
sense of what can be done with reason and honour and
without the condemnation of mankind. This is plain
already from what he says about sanctions, and becomes
more obvious still when he writes 'I must retrace my steps
and must deprive those who wage war of nearly all the

principles which I seemed to grant, yet did not grant, to them.' For what is *allowed* (in the sense of what can be *done with impunity*) includes many dishonourable and unjust actions.

In Grotius's work the term *natural law* straddles law as generalization, law as custom and law as injunction. Natural law is discovered partly by reason (including reasoning about what kind of creature God made in making man and about what God wants man to do); it is also discovered by observing the actual character of human deeds. Thus, natural law is to some extent a matter of generalization about actualities, yet at the same time those actualities concern creatures whose behaviour can be governed by reason and fear of God. Grotius treats civil laws as injunctions based on reason and created by man; on the law of nations, however, he is less clear. At first he stresses its similarity to civil law and argues, as we have seen, that there can be at least some effective law – both civil and international – in the absence of sanctions. Later he says that international law 'allows' everything and forbids nothing; here perhaps he is thinking of natural law as made up of generalizations about what men do and not about what they think. Finally he retraces his steps, as he puts it, and deprives those who wage war of many of their 'principles' by setting out what is permissible and not permissible according to the injunctions of reason and honour.

Customary ways of thinking and the injunctions of reason and honour, he says, tell us that no war can be justly waged if the original reason for starting it was a bad one. Even in a war fought for the best reasons the right to kill and destroy is restricted. For instance, there is a limit, dictated by reason, on vengeance and punishment. No-one can be justly punished except for his own misdeeds, hence communities can only be reasonably punished for the actions of their rulers if they agreed to those actions. What a community *owns* can be passed on by inheritance to its new generations but what it *deserves* is not heritable. So it is unjust to punish the descendants of those who have

wronged you, as Alexander claimed to punish the Persians.
The intentional killing of the innocent – Grotius here lists
children, women, old men, clerics, and literary men like
himself – is never justified; it is better to spare the guilty
than to kill the innocent even by accident or as a side-effect.
It is wrong to kill or torture hostages or prisoners of war.
Fair offers of surrender should be accepted and the terms
honoured. Those who surrender unconditionally should
have their lives spared. Even the guilty should not be killed
if their number is very great. Crops should not be
devastated except in cases of dire necessity; holy places
(churches and the like) and works of art should never be
destroyed, since they are not part of the enemy's armaments and their destruction helps no-one. Those enslaved
should not be killed or tortured, for slaves are human
beings and there is a kind of blood link between all the
members of a single species which is respected even by
dumb animals. Neutral states should not be harmed, nor
should their goods be taken except for reasons of dire
necessity. Good faith in truces must be kept with enemies of
every description, including tyrants, pirates, rebels and
revolutionaries. Guarantees of safe conduct must be faith-
fully adhered to. Finally, peace must be sought always,
even if it sometimes involves loss.

The briefest statement of the theory of the just war is a
list of three conditions: just cause, just means, proper
authority. These conditions are jointly sufficient and
severally necessary for justice in war. Yet war is such an
evil that even the completest justice cannot by itself alone
provide reason for fighting. Often the best action is to seek
peace, not justice. This is certainly Grotius's opinion; and
even the staunchest anti-pacifist must allow that sometimes
peace is more important than justice.

7

Guilt and Innocence

In the theory of the just war the justice of means and methods is not a relative matter. An unjust method of warfare – for example, one that involves killing the innocent – is unjust *per se*. Justice does not depend on what your enemy is doing: the theory does not allow the argument 'He is killing my innocent non-combatants so I may, in just retaliation, kill his innocent non-combatants'.

The theory is vulnerable to the objection that the distinction it draws between the innocent, who ought not to be attacked, and the guilty, who may be, cannot coincide with a distinction between legitimate and non-legitimate targets. For on any ordinary understanding of the terms *innocent* and *guilty* so many people will count as innocent that war itself turns out to be illicit and the just war theory collapses into pacifism.

If we collect together the ideas of Aquinas, Vitorio and Grotius we obtain quite a long list of types of innocent persons, comprising rulers of states engaged in just wars; soldiers fighting in just wars – that is, those fighting on the morally right side; rulers who after serious deliberation and after taking counsel from wise men come to the sincere, though false, belief that their cause is just; ordinary soldiers on the morally wrong side who are not close to government and so cannot know that their rulers are in the wrong; children ('even the children of Turks'); women (unless they have power in the state or have committed crimes); old men (with the same proviso); and all harmless unarmed folk such as peasants, clerics, and literary men.

Guilt as it is understood in civil law requires in general an objective injury or wrong and either a guilty mind or culpable negligence. If this somewhat complex notion is transferred to warfare, then it is easy to argue that many rulers and most ordinary soldiers on both sides are innocent. Vitorio in fact argues in just this way.

However, this account of guilt and innocence cannot be combined with *both* a ban on the direct killing of the innocent *and* and acceptance of a just war theory. The three items form an inconsistent triad.

If all the soldiers on the morally right side are thereby innocent, then to kill them is murder and on a par with killing children (say). Those on the morally wrong side who cannot know that their rulers are engaged in an unjust war are also innocent, and to kill *them* is murder and on a par with killing helpless old peasants, or priests, or nuns. Rulers, who after due consultation and after taking counsel from wise men come to believe sincerely, albeit wrongly, that their cause for war is a just cause, are also innocent; to kill them, if one could get hold of them, would be murder. But who then *may* be killed in a just war justly fought? Only those few rulers who have either failed to take proper consultation (negligence) or who know themselves that their cause is not just (guilty mind). But a war with so few protagonists is not a war at all.

On killing the innocent, G. E. M. Anscombe writes: 'The principal wickedness which is a temptation to those engaged in warfare is the killing of the inocent, which may often be done with impunity and even to the glory of those who do it . . . the commander, and especially the conqueror, massacres people by the thousand, either because this is part of his glory, or as a terrorizing measure, or as part of his tactics.' Well, who is innocent and who guilty? Anscombe says 'in international warfare . . . the charac-terisation of (the) enemy as non-innocent has not been ratified by legal process. This however does not mean that the notion of innocence fails in this situation. What is required, for the people attacked to be non-innocent in the relevant sense, is that they should themselves be engaged in an objectively unjust proceeding which the attacker has the right to make his concern; or – the commonest case – should be unjustly attacking him.'[1]

This account of non-innocence allows that those fighting on the right side do not commit murder when they kill the soldiers fighting on the wrong side. On the other hand, since non-innocence is characterized by being engaged in an objectively unjust proceeding, it follows that when those on the wrong side kill the soldiers who are *not* engaged in an objectively unjust proceeding – i.e., those on the morally right side – they act just as badly as if they were to kill unarmed women and children, for they are killing the non-non-innocent, i.e., the innocent. I am not sure that Anscombe can have intended this conclusion but it seems to follow all the same.

How to get out of this tangle? Does the trouble arise because of the idea that 'acting under orders' can absolve the ordinary soldier from guilt? The view that war is a kind of extension of internal jurisdiction strongly encourages the supposition that the ordinary citizen has a positive duty to fight in war if ordered to do so, just as he has a duty to obey the laws of his country. Now if he is acting according to duty, then he is not acting unjustly. So all soldiers are innocent, and to kill them is murder. (This is strangely akin to the pacifist position.) But let us now suppose for the sake of argument that the citizen has no duty to fight when told to unless the cause is objectively just, and also that it is the citizen's own job to find out to the best of his ability whether that is so, and that when he cannot find out, then he ought not to obey his rulers but should place on them the onus of proof. If we suppose all this, then the soldiers fighting on the wrong side are probably most of them guilty in one way or another: guilty either of failing to find out about the causes of the war or of knowingly engaging in an objectively unjust proceeding or of failing to stand up to unjust rulers. And so *those* soldiers may be killed without committing murder. But no distinction has yet been made between killing innocent soldiers and killing unarmed civilians, and it remains the case that on the account given of non-innocence there will be in any war quite large numbers of innocent soldiers, to wit, all those on the morally right side. The only way of avoiding the conclusion that killing the soldiers who are on the right side is the same sort of thing as killing unarmed civilians is either to re-define innocence and non-innocence more radically than Anscombe has done, or to drop these notions and construct a distinction in some other way.

Soldiers carry arms, they are therefore dangerous. Shall we say that innocent just means *harmless*, and guilty, or non-innocent, just means *dangerous*? Then it will be all right to kill soldiers – much as it is all right to kill wild beasts. Well, this does draw a distinction between killing a soldier and killing an unarmed man or a child: but does it draw it in the right way? We seem to have lost the ideas of justice and injustice. But how can we retain the theory of the just war if we cannot say that the protagonists on the unjust side are unjust? The suggested re-definition is too radical.

Military men have professional military duties which include killing soldiers. Soldiers can be guilty of crime in war, but killing the soldiers on the other side is not a crime unless those killed are prisoners, say, or in hospital. The professional status of a soldier on this account is *sui generis*, allowing him to be rightly killed even though he has done no wrong, and allowing him in turn to kill (and rightly) those who like himself are soldiers and who also may be doing no wrong. This way out of the tangle again relies on a new definition of innocence and guilt. We have, as it were, discovered a *sui generis* variety of innocent person who can be killed without the killing being murder.

It seems that we will have to conclude, *pro tem*, that the thesis that the innocent must not be directly attacked in war, the thesis that a just war is possible, and the thesis that the distinction between guilt and innocence has an ordinary and straightforward application to those who engage in war form an inconsistent triad. Then which of the theses must be given up? To give up the first is to give up a central tenet of the just war theory, to give up the second is to give up the just war theory itself. Giving up the third leads, *via* arbitrary definitions, to intolerable theoretical quandaries.

Some authors have decided that it may be best to stop trying to establish the criteria for guilt and innocence in war and concentrate instead on the legal notions used by those who draw up international treaties designed to mitigate the cruelties of war. Thus Nicholas Denyer writes 'the greater a distinction's failures in sharpness and visbility the less use it can have in a legal system . . . above all, in the law of war, where the nice adjudication of civil life will obviously be impossible, the sharp and visible distinction between combatants and non-combatants is exactly what one needs'.[2]

Well, how can combatant and non-combatant be best defined? Should all non-combatants be immune from attack? Are all combatants legitimate targets?

A serving soldier is a paradigm example of a legitimate target. If it is not legitimate to kill soldiers in war it can hardly be legitimate to kill anyone else. A soldier, surely, must expect to be treated as a target. However, not all soldiers are combatants and few soldiers are combatants all the time. Of those who are not combatants, some are and some are not legitimate targets. Also, some non-soldiers are at least borderline combatants.

Non-combatant soldiers include army doctors, injured soldiers in field hospitals, and prisoners of war. It is generally agreed that none of these are legitimate targets. Indeed, attacking field hospitals or hospital ships and killing prisoners of war are war crimes.[3] Unarmed senior officers, on the other hand, are surely legitimate targets even if these days they no longer lead troops into battle. If they are immune from attack in practice, that may be in part the result of a trade unionism of generals.

Spies and informers are not always members of the armed forces, and even when they are (secretly), their job need not involve killing people. Spies, especially if they are also traitors, are generally regarded as criminals rather than as combatants, and a legitimate target is not necessarily the same thing as a criminal except perhaps in the just war theory itself. Again, in guerrilla war the distinction between a legitimate target and a criminal may be impossible to draw in practice. In any case, surely a spy is a legitimate target if he cannot be captured and tried.

An informer is a kind of spy who works either for the police or, in a conquered or colonized country, for the conquering power. Whether an informer is a legitimate target seems to me to depend on circumstances, including the nature of the information he collects. But if an informer works for a conquering power or for a government of tyrants and gangsters, he must surely expect to become a target and most would agree, I think, that such a man is a legitimate target.

Politicians *per se* are not combatants but it is they who initiate wars and who decide to continue them. It is they who are responsible for conscription. It is they who in the end are responsible for the ways in which wars are fought – Harry Truman is a dramatic example. Surely, then, they can sometimes be legitimate targets of attack.

It may be that we need to rely on more than one kind of difference in order to draw a satisfactory line between legitimate and non-legitimate targets.

8

Self-Defence

If there is no right of self-defence there can be no sound theory of justice in war. Now, as it happens, the just war theorists of the Middle Ages were less concerned with wars of defence than with wars of attack. This can be seen from what they say about just causes in general, and also from the advice given to princes. Princes were advised to take counsel from wise men, to think very carefully and calmly, and in general to be very hesitant about embarking on war; now this advice is most suitable for those not already under attack. For the philosophers and theologians of the Middle Ages, self-defence was only one of several possible just causes and, generally speaking, they gave it rather less attention than the others. They certainly believed that a war of attack can be just and right: it is so when, for example, it has the character of punishment, or of a measure needed to prevent the conversion of Christians to paganism or heresy, or is waged in order to retrieve stolen land or property. The idea that warlike aggression is *eo ipso* wrong is partly the result of pacifist ideas and partly a product of the ever-increasing scale of warfare.

Self-defence is given little attention by just war theorists for the further reason that the individual's right to defend himself from mortal threat was taken for granted. There is, however, an incoherency in post-Augustine Christian thought on this point, for on the one hand the right to wage defensive war is taken to rest on, and indeed to be the same kind of thing as, a supposedly self-evident right of individuals to use force or even to kill as a means to self-defence: yet on the other hand the Gospel injunctions *not* to use force, it is argued, apply only to individuals and not to states. Thus the right to make defensive *war* rests, for a Christian, on a non-existent right of the *individual* to use force in self-defence.

Is there a right to self-defence? Does it extend to defence of property as well as persons? Is it limited or unlimited? And if limited, then what do the limits relate to?

One surely has a right when no other people are involved to defend oneself without limit and as one sees fit against natural and mechanical dangers such as falling rocks, flood and fire, and empty runaway railway trains; also against germs and viruses and savage wild beasts. The right to self-defence, and its limits, are only really contentious matters when the dangers to the self-defender are posed by other human beings.

From the point of view of the self-defender people who pose a danger to life are of several kinds. There are those who do so deliberately and knowingly and with the intention of harming and killing him (for example, a would-be assassin, or the public hangman). There are those who do so deliberately and knowingly but without the intention of harming the self-defender (for example, a policeman who fires a gun at a criminal standing next to the self-defender). There are those who do so unknowingly and *ergo* without any intention to harm anyone (for example, a child who throws a hand grenade which he believes is a toy). There are 'innocent shields', that is, those whose unwilling presence prevents the self-defender from exercising direct force on an attacker. The last three types of danger are sometimes called 'innocent attacks'. Lastly, an attack made by an agent of the community (such as a police officer) while doing his duty is not normally thought of as criminal: hence it is possible for an attacker to be in the right.

In what follows I shall describe what the traditional

teachings of Judaism and of the Catholic Church have to say about innocent and non-innocent attackers; and then proceed to discuss the views of a number of twentieth-century philosophers.

Traditional Jewish teaching on self-defence against human attackers begins from the proposition that murder is the worst possible offence.[1] Killing is, of course, prohibited by one of the Ten Commandments, but the death penalty is prescribed only for wilful murder; in biblical times accidental killers took asylum in cities of refuge. Any death resulting from an illegal assault counts as murder, whether or not the attacker intends the death of his victim. Non-murderous homicide is categorized as either justifiable or excusable. Justifiable homicide is either permissible or obligatory. Killing a burglar at night (for example) is permissible, the presumption being, when this rule was laid down, that the burglar would otherwise kill the householder. Killing a burglar by daylight is not permissible because in the daytime it is possible to call in help and also one can see the thief and judge what he is up to. The killing of criminals by officers deputed to that task by the authorities is obligatory, but a failure to carry out the obligation – as would happen if, for example, the public hangman went on strike – is not a punishable crime. The rule no doubt stems from the arrangements made when everyone was in effect a public executioner, namely, when the death penalty consisted in being stoned to death by the whole community.

There is in traditional Jewish law a positive obligation to rescue others from immediate death or rape. If any person, including an infant, pursues another with the manifest intention to kill him, anyone present has a duty to rescue the victim, even to killing the pursuer. (This rule has been extended to killing an embryo in order to save the mother's life, and to killing a would-be rapist immediately before he carries out his crime). On the other hand, it would be as unlawful to kill the pursuer if the victim could be rescued by other means as it would be not to kill the pursuer if the victim could not otherwise be rescued.

The right to self-defence has been only partly superseded by legal redress – that is, it survives in that it is all right to take the law into your own hands if the civil authorities cannot save you. There remains a positive duty of rescue.

There are four offences of which it is held that a Jew must allow himself to be killed rather than commit. These are idolatry, murder, incest and adultery. If a man commits murder because he is himself under direct threat of death he sins reprehensibly, but he is not held criminally responsible, for it is irrevocably presumed that when a man acts under threat of immediate death in order to save his life any criminal intent on his part is excluded or superceded. His action is therefore excusable though not justifiable. Other excusable homicides are those committed by persons under real threat of being tortured, or by infants below the age of responsibility (12 and 13), or by lunatics. Unlike all other legal systems, traditional Jewish law allows ignorance, and ignorance of the law, as a plea. Mistakes of fact count as a kind of duress, called 'duress of the heart', and duress can be pleaded to absolve one of criminal responsibility. However, it is held that a normal person could not mistakenly believe that homicide is permitted.

Traditional Roman Catholic teaching on self-defence is as follows: man has a natural inalienable inviolable right to life, which, however, has certain 'intrinsic limitations' which follow from society's right to punish serious crimes with death. The right to life carries with it the right to preserve one's life against unjust attacks, but only by means which are not intrinsically evil. It is possible to violate another's rights involuntarily as well as voluntarily, and self-defence is equally legitimate in either case. But there are limits to this right. One's motive must be to defend oneself rather than to harm the attacker. Force must be used only at the time of the attack; to use force beforehand would be aggression, and to use it afterwards is revenge. Force is not permissible if escape is possible. It is not permissible to use more than the minimum force needed to prevent or ward off the attack. The use of force is not intrinsically evil provided these four conditions are observed. The right to self-defence includes the right to kill an unjust aggressor if that is the only means of stopping him. There is a *right* but not a *duty* of self-defence; failure to exercise the right is therefore not equivalent to suicide. The right extends to the protection of property since goods and property are necessary for life.

The theory that the right to self-defence rests on the natural right to life has recently been challenged by Judith Jarvis Thomson. She imagines a case in which Aggressor means to kill another man, Victim, by running him down with a tank. Victim has an anti-tank gun which could destroy the tank, though not without killing Aggressor; but, says Thomson: 'Aggressor is a human being; so he, like the rest of us has a right to life, and presumably, therefore, the right not to be killed . . . . Precisely *why* is it permissible for Victim to use that anti-tank gun on Aggressor?'[2]

Thus, according to Thomson, there is a difficulty about explaining the right to self-defence even in the cases in which one defends oneself against the deliberate wrongful harm-intending actions of men who set out to kill. The Utilitarian answer, that the life of the innocent party is of more social value than that of the guilty party, will not do, firstly because it is not always true, secondly because anyway the social value of a whole life cannot be known before it is over, thirdly because that which is inalienable surely cannot be rightly overriden by other considerations.

Thomson suggests we distinguish between the violation of a right and an infringement of a right. In self-defence Victim does not violate Aggressor's right to life if he kills him, but merely infringes it. This, it seems to me, won't solve the problem unless *infringe* is re-defined. For normally *infringe* and *violate* mean much the same thing. To infringe means to break, injure or damage something, and an *infringement* is a breach or violation of a law or a right; to violate means to break, transgress or infringe. *Violation*, unlike *infringement*, is etymologically associated with *violence*, but since abstract entities may be violated it is possible to violate without the use of physical force. Thus, as Tennyson said 'The press easily violates virgin truth for a coin or a cheque'. In Thomson's story, when Victim blasts Aggressor's tank with his gun, his infringement of Aggressor's right to life involves violence anyway and, because both infringements and violations are breaches or transgressions, this particular infringement seems to be *prima facie* indistinguishable from a violation.

Thomson, though, does re-define *infringement*, as follows: If someone has a right that p be the case (where p is a proposition describing a state of affairs) then we infringe his right if we make p false. We violate his right if our making p false is wrongful.[2] She then argues, *via* examples, that not all infringements are violations, though some are. The notion that all infringements are violations is the notion that every right is *absolute*.

It seems to me that her distinction is not helpful, for two reasons. First, it leaves open the question whether a right that has been infringed (whether rightly or wrongly) continues to exist. If it does, then it looks as if infringement is always wrong. On the other hand, if infringement has the effect of cancelling a right, then infringement is always right. Second, the distinction otherwise seems to boil down to saying that infringement is permissible when it is permissible and not when not: a circularity noted by Thomson herself.

The problem is sometimes attacked by saying that an aggressor *forfeits* his right to life when he tries to kill a victim. But it has been argued, against this, that the use of the term *forfeit* in this context is an extended or analogical one.[3] The legal idea of forfeit relates to material possessions and also to incorporeal goods of a kind that can be lost or transferred, such as citizenship. If a man's right has been forfeited in law this may or may not be as a result of his own actions. Thus one's citizenship might be forfeit simply because of a change in the laws of the land. In the past the status of outlaw was of one whose right to life was forfeit. The status was conferred by the king and his ministers and could be conferred on one who had done no wrong, like the Robin Hood of legend. When a man loses a legal right by forfeiture, the knowledge or ignorance of the putative violator of the (now non-existent) right – and even indeed his intentions – are irrelevant to the legality of the deed. Thus when a rogue publisher publishes your book not knowing that your copyright has been forfeited but rather intending to do you down and make a huge profit which will cover all possible damages and legal expenses, then if your copyright has in fact already been forfeited you cannot sue him. Similarly, no-one killing Robin Hood in ignorance of his outlaw status would have been guilty of a crime. It is quite otherwise with the victim who putatively violates an aggressor's right to life, for in law the justification of self-defence requires a proper intention. The self-defender must know that he is threatened, and must act in good faith. Now, if the aggressor had forfeited his right to life in the legal sense of forfeit, there would be no need for the victim to have either knowledge or right intentions.

Thomson's problem stems from the idea of *rights*. The problem is posed in terms of rights: if every human being has a natural, inviolable, inalienable right to life, how can it be permissible to kill, even in self-defence? How can an aggressor's actions remove his irremovable rights?

Well, is all talk of natural rights just 'nonsense on stilts', perhaps? It has to be admitted that in ordinary use, which in case of this particular word is largely political use, much talk of rights *per se*, let alone natural rights, is polluted by pomposity and wind-baggery. Nevertheless there *is* a coherent concept of natural rights.

Natural rights and moral rights contrast with legal rights. Someone who violates or infringes another's legal right acts illegally. If the legal system is sensible, just and decent, many violations of legal right will also be violations of moral right. It probably goes without saying that the existence of a legal right does not guarantee the existence of a moral right and may, in fact, enshrine injustice. Conversely, there are moral rights which are not enforced by law.

Natural rights are a type of moral right. Now some moral rights presuppose the existence of legal institutions. For instance, if a cruel father cuts his dutiful son out of his will in a country which allows full testamentary freedom, then the son (we say) may still have a moral right to the estate even though he has no legal right to it. Still, his moral right in this case presupposes the existence of wills and heritable property. Contrariwise, in asserting the existence of a natural right, one presupposes nothing about the existence of legal or other conventional institutions: this is one of the marks of a natural right. Secondly, natural rights are not particular, that is, they do not belong to some individuals and not to others. Natural rights belong to human beings as such and therefore to all human beings.

The concept of a natural right, it seems to me, is perfectly coherent. As to the old debate about whether this coherent concept has any instances, is it not entirely fruitless?

Because natural rights belong to all members of the human race they are relatively few, and for this and perhaps other reasons they are liable to be defined extensionally; that is, by a list. The best-known lists are (1) Life, Liberty and the Pursuit of Happiness, and (2) Life, Liberty and Property. It is not clear whether (3) Liberty, Equality, Fraternity, is supposed to be a list of *rights*. Natural rights are thought of as stemming from the very essence or nature of mankind as a species which must mean that the traditional lists are too short. For instance, it seems intuitively obvious that people have a right to reproduce themselves if they want to, and that this is part of their nature. If this is not a natural right, then nothing is and we had better say straight off that the concept is empty after all. In a two-sex species, reproduction (of course) requires the co-operation of another individual. Therefore the natural right to reproduce oneself cannot be absolute in the sense that one may do whatever one believes to be necessary to exercise one's right. The right, though natural, does not override the natural right of other people to liberty (say). If the right were absolute in the sense adumbrated above, then rape, random imprisonment, kidnapping, and so on, would all be in principle permissible. But surely the natural right of reproduction does not carry with it a right to perpetrate rape, nor does it necessarily justify polygamy and polyandry.

Now, can a right be inalienable and inviolable yet not absolute?

Inalienable means non-transferable. Legal rights can be transferred by sales, contracts, divorces, and so on. For they belong to a person in the first place because of an institutional status, such as owner, husband, etc., and one can divest oneself of a merely institutional status. Natural rights belong to individuals in virtue of their membership of the human race; one cannot divest oneself of one's membership of the human race except by ceasing to exist altogether. Natural rights cannot be transferred because any being capable of holding a natural right already has it; cannot (as it were) hold it twice over; and hence cannot be given it. On the other hand, an entity which lacks natural rights does so because it is incapable of holding them and hence, for that different reason, cannot be given them. Thus you cannot transfer your natural rights to David himself, nor can you transfer them to a statue of David. Can non-transferable rights be *lost*? There is a dilemma here, for it looks as if we must either say that one can lose one's natural rights without losing one's nature (which sounds absurd), or say that all cases of the over-riding of natural rights are thereby violations, and that all natural rights are in some sense absolute; which also seems absurd, though in a different way. Let us then look at the idea of *violation*.

Inviolable is a normative term meaning not to be violated; to be kept sacred from infraction. Compare *inviolate*, which means that which is not or cannot in fact be violated. An inviolable right is not an inviolate right, indeed there are no inviolate rights, no rights which are never violated. How could there be? Mankind is not so angelic.

What is an inviolable right? Plainly one which ought not to be violated. But that must be true of any moral right. There aren't any moral rights which *ought* to be violated! Yet on the other hand it is common enough in the law that one man's right is held to be (rightly) over-ridden by another's more important right. Is over-riding to count as violation? Or does an over-ridden right lapse or even cease to exist? In the case of legal rights any of these answers could be the right one, depending on the context. The state, after all, can change its laws and in so doing it might abolish some rights; it can declare states of emergency, thus making some rights lapse for a time; or it can ignore its own rules, and thereby violate rights it has itself created.

In the case of moral rights it seems to me that the natural thing to say is that when a lesser right ought, in a particular case, to be over-ridden by a greater, then its holder loses (at least temporarily) the moral right in question. No doubt readers will be able to think up hard cases in which it is *not* natural to say this; but for the moment anyway this looks like the correct answer. An example: the ethical code of doctors demands that they do not divulge details of their patients' illnesses or private lives to third parties. It is taken that patients have a moral right to confidentiality. In the nineteenth century, when syphilis was incurable, doctors were sometimes bothered by what to do about the possible syphilitic patient who insisted on getting married while refusing to tell his bride-to-be about his disease.[4] As nowadays in the case of the disease known as AIDS, the spokesmen of the medical profession placed some emphasis on the possible practical difficulties that would follow upon a breach of the rule of confidentiality. That is, it was argued that if secrecy were not assured patients would not seek medical help and thus might spread the disease amongst the community. This point of view, however, says nothing about patients' rights; and it ignores the rights of others in that it appears to treat brides and wives not only as non-members of the community but as beings who have no right to expect the medical profession to directly protect them from an avoidable mortal illness. I think that most people not in love with secrecy would hold that the third party's right to the knowledge essential for protecting herself (or himself) from a mortal illness over-rides the patient's right to confidentiality in this case, and also over-rides any realistic practical considerations. Even doctors would agree to that if the third party in question were herself a doctor or a doctor's daughter or sister. Does the patient's right still exist, though over-ridden? Surely the answer is No.

What about natural rights? When a self-defender kills an aggressor who by his actions has obviously been threatening death, does he violate the aggressor's natural right to life? Has the aggressor's right been rightly or wrongly over-ridden? What are we to say about its putatively continuing existence and its putative violation? Let us remember that *inviolable* does not mean *cannot be violated* nor *is not violated (inviolate)*. The word is normative, and since it is absurd to say 'unlike other moral rights, natural rights ought not to be violated' what it must mean is: *ought not be over-ridden by other rights*.

What of conflicts *between* natural rights? Should one natural right (liberty, say) be allowed to over-ride another (property, say)? As soon as this question is asked it becomes obvious that these two rights cannot be inviolable *vis-a-vis* each other. It cannot be that X's right to property may never be over-ridden by Y's right to liberty. And it cannot be that X's right to liberty may never be over-ridden by Y's right to liberty. If such over-ridings are violations our talk of rights comes perilously close to being nonsensical. In brief, setting aside the right to life, to which I return below, a natural right cannot be inviolable *if that means* it may never be over-ridden, not even by itself (as it were) or by another natural right. Second, if an individual's natural or other moral right has been properly over-ridden, it may be best to regard it as having ceased to exist; if it is a natural right, then temporarily; if it is another kind of moral right, possibly permanently. This may sound rather vague, but we are at this point dealing with one of those philosophical problems that in the end are solved by hitting on a lucky word. We need a lucky word to describe what goes on when an inalienable right (for instance, the right to liberty) is properly over-ridden – as it obviously can be. Unfortunately *lapsing* and *ceasing* are not lucky enough but I cannot think of anything better. Still it is plain that the cases under consideration are distinguishable from those in which a right is *improperly* over-ridden, when it is best to say that it continues to exist though violated.

The right to life is unique. To say that the right to life is of supreme and fundamental importance is something of a *façon de parler*. It cannot be measured on a scale against the other natural rights, for, as Kant might have said, life is the ground of all rights whatsoever: so that the right to life is the right to the ground of all other rights. However one expresses it, life (and the right to it) is categorically different from liberty, property or happiness and the right to those.

Secondly, the right to life seems to be a Hohfeldian liberty-right. This shows up in the implications of the right to kill in self-defence.

Consider the right to defend yourself against someone who makes a deliberate, harm-intending, possibly deadly attack on you. Most authors assume that anyone who makes a deliberate and harm-intending attack is automatically in the wrong. Just as *violence* is sometimes re-defined to mean wrongful force (or even just wrongful anything), so *attack* is often taken to mean *wrongful* attack. In a way, this is a tribute to the power of pacifist arguments, because it implies that, in the case of war at least, simply to take the first step is overwhelmingly wrong. All the same, not all deliberate harm-intending attacks are wrong. Generally speaking, traditional philosophy allows that officers of the state (policemen, hangmen) who kill in the course of doing their duty are innocent of crime or sin; though to my mind too many of the world's police forces behave like the Ton Ton Macoute for this to be a satisfactory intellectual position. Still, there are many cases of deliberate attack which have more intuitive appeal than the behaviour of the Ton Ton. If (in Britain, say) an escaped convict commits some murders and then seizes a hostage, a police sharp-hooter firing at him with the intention of harming and even killing him is surely not acting wrongly. Nor can we pretend that his action is not an *attack* on the convict.

Does a self-defender have a right to kill one who makes a deliberate and probably deadly attack on him when that is the only way of saving his own life (a) when the attacker acts rightfully, and (b) when the attacker acts wrongfully? if the answer is Yes in the first case, (a), then I think we can take it that the answer is also Yes in the second case, (b). Alas, the answer is far from obvious in either case.

Consider Robert Nozick's treatment of the question. First he says 'the principle that prohibits physical aggression . . . does not prohibit the use of force in defense against another party who is a threat, even though he is innocent and deserves no retribution . . . libertarian principles [i.e., Nozick's own] are usually formulated so as to forbid using violence on innocent persons. But innocent threats . . . are another matter to which different principles must apply'. In the same book he writes: '. . . whether someone wrongfully attacking (or participating in the attack of) another may claim self-defense as justifying his killing the other when the other, in self-defense, acts so as to endanger his own attacker's life . . . the answer is "No". The attacker should not be attacking in the first place, nor does someone else's threatening him with death unless he does attack make it permissible for him to do so . . . soldiers who know their country is waging an aggressive war and who are manning anti-aircraft guns in defense of a military emplacement may *not* fire upon the planes of the attacked nation which is acting in self-defense even if the planes are over their heads and about to bomb them'.[5]

Nozick's first position is that it is all right for an innocent man to kill an innocent shield; and his second position is that it is not all right for a guilty man to kill an innocent attacker. In other words, a currently innocent man acquires no guilt in killing an innocent threat, but an already guilty man acquires extra guilt in doing so. But how can this be? It looks absurd. Still, that is not our concern. Let us compare his second passage with Thomas Hobbes's contrary opinion: '. . . there be some Rights, which no man can be understood by any words or other signes, to have abandoned, or transferred. As first, a man cannot lay down the right of resisting them that assault him by force, to take away his life . . .' and: 'A Covenant not to defend my selfe from force, by force, is always voyd . . . And this is granted to be true by all men, in that they lead Criminals to

Execution, and Prison, with armed men . . .' and: 'A Covenant to accuse onselfe, without assurance of pardon, is invalide . . .'.[6]

Nozick's (second) view perhaps stems from a common semi-conscious assumption that self-defence incorporates punishment. Augustine's idea that killing in war or peace is justified when it punishes wrong-doers may be partly responsible for the prevalence of this assumption. (Evidence for its existence can be seen in the invention of such technical terms as '*objectively* unjust', used to describe actions which are unintentionally or accidentally harmful). The assumption is not confined to Christian thinkers, however. There is a nice example in Jewish traditional law: according to one of its rulings it was decided that some sailors who threw a donkey overboard in order to lighten a sinking boat acted rightfully because the donkey by being in the boat was objectively engaging in an unwarranted attack on their lives.[7]

It seems to me that in cases where life itself is at stake Hobbes is right and Nozick is wrong, but I cannot for the moment see any way of proving this. Hobbes's own arguments are not conclusive and Nozick does not give any arguments.

If an individual under immediate threat of death from another retains his right to defend himself whatever the rights and wrongs of the original quarrel, it follows that at some point in the fight both the defender and the attacker may well have an equal right to try to kill the other. In other cases the right not to have something done to you, or to have something happen, entails an obligation on the part of others. Anscombe's account of rights as 'stopping modals' aptly illustrates the general belief that 'N has the right . . .' means the same as 'Others may not, e.g., stop him from . . .'.[8] Is the right to life an exception to this? Phillip Montague, writing precisely about the right to life itself, says: '. . . it seems to me quite clear that the right not to be killed and the obligation to refrain from killing are logically on a par, and, in fact, the same concept viewed from two different standpoints. X's right not to be killed by

Y is nothing more than Y's obligation to refrain from killing X'.[9]

Yet if Hobbes's opinion is the correct one, the right to life is not like this. It might be thought anomalous to have to say that in self-defence situations two men have an equal right to life and yet neither acts wrongly in trying to defend himself by killing the other. But that just seems to be what the right to life is like.

'Innocent threats' are of several kinds. There is the rightful attacker (such as the police marksman in my earlier example); the deranged lunatic who intends an attack but (as we say) 'does not know what he is doing'; the individual who has no intention of making an attack (for example, one who playfully tosses hand grenades at you, thinking they are toys); and there is the 'innocent shield' or hostage, one who unwillingly stands between an attacker and a self-defender.

Hobbes discusses only attackers: he believes that the right of self-defence extends to killing even rightful attackers such as the public hangman. It is not possible to say what he would have thought about killing innocent threats who do not intend to attack, but it possibly appears to follow from his principles that one may do so. Jewish teaching allows the killing of a few types of innocent threat, but each type is treated separately and on its merits and there is no inference that one may kill any and all kinds of innocent threat. Catholic teaching is that it is all right to defend oneself by force against either formal or material aggression or injustice. *Formal* means voluntary, and *material*, involuntary injustice. There is nothing wrong with the term 'involuntary injustice', and no doubt there is a sense in which people perpetrate injustices involuntarily every day; but the fact that the idea makes sense does not provide a reason for harming those who commit such injustices. Contrariwise, the very definition of *material injustice* incorporates a *prima facie* reason for *not* harming them. The introduction of a distinction between the formal and the material is a kind of verbal manoeuvre. One might as well try to justify punishing innocent people by inventing a distinction between *formal* and *material* punishment – the latter expression to mean the punishment of those who have done no wrong.

Montague says that self-defence cases 'involving innocent aggressors, accidental threats, and innocent bystanders, are all in very much the same moral boat'. He argues that it is *permissible* to kill in such cases, while in self-defence situations 'brought about by culpably aggressive or threatening behavior' one has a *right* to kill.[10] But surely one must have a *right* anyway to do whatever is *permissible*? To think otherwise, it seems to me, is to treat *rights* as a magic word. The permissibility of killing innocent threats is, in any case, no light matter. It would appear that the distinction between permissibility and right is being made to bear more moral weight than it can carry.

Montague makes a potentially more valuable distinction when he points out that not all cases of self-preservation are cases of self-defence. It was suggested in chapter four that a stipulative definition or distinction need not be either surreptitious or arbitrary. Let us distinguish, though not in an arbitrary way, between self-defence and self-preservation. Let us define acts of self-defence as a sub-set of acts of self-preservation. Let us further define acts of self-defence as being those acts of self-preservation which presuppose an immediate threat from an agent who intends (for good reasons or bad) to kill or seriously injure you, and which themselves consist of immediate counter-attacks directed at that agent and at no-one else.

This definition excludes some but not all killing of innocent threats. One can (logically) act in self-defence, as defined above, against a rightful attacker such as the police marksman in our earlier story. What about G. P. Fletcher's celebrated Psychotic Aggressor?[11] Well, he (PA) is after all an aggressor, and his intentions are clear enough – he wants to kill the victim of his attack. Possibly PA is labouring under the delusion that the victim himself has intentions which he does not have, or that he is a person that he is not – Mussolini, say, or a member of the Anti-Lunatic Fringe. But still, PA does really intend to kill the victim 'under the description of' Mussolini (or whatever). Hence it is logically possible to act in self-defence, as defined above, against the Psychotic Agressor.

On the other hand, one cannot (logically cannot) kill an innocent bystander or an innocent shield in self-defence as now defined. For innocent bystanders and innocent shields do not make attacks; they merely get in the way. To intentionally kill an innocent bystander or an innocent shield might be an act of self-preservation but it is not necessarily an act of self-defence. Our question about killing innocent threats now resolves itself into two:

(1) Is the right to self-defence absolute or relative?

(2) Is the right to self-preservation (excluding acts of self-defence) absolute or relative?

As regards (1), it seems to me that the correct (Hobbesian) answer to the first question is that the right to self-defence, as now defined, is absolute.

As regards (2), it seems to me that the right to preserve oneself in situations not involving the need for self-defence, is relative. It has many limits, imposed upon it by reason.

There are four grounds for thinking that the right to self-defence is absolute while the right to self-preservation is relative. First, this conclusion, taken together with the analysis given of *inviolable inalienable rights*, will, I think, turn out to provide answers to the puzzles posed by Judith Jarvis Thomson. Second, it accords with our moral intuition that killing innocent bystanders simply cannot be on a par with killing attackers, however well-justified, or, alternatively, however deluded those attackers might happen to be. Third, the answers it gives to dilemmas about action accord at least roughly with the answers given by the traditional moral teaching of two highly developed codes, namely Catholicism and Judaism. Fourth, it accounts for what the law and our moral intuitions tell us about what it is right for third parties to do. In the case of an innocent victim directly threatened by an attacker and at the same time indirectly 'threatened' by the attacker's innocent hostage, or by an innocent bystander, a third party has no obligation to try to save the victim of the threat by killing the hostage or the bystander. Nor, of course, does he have an obligation to try to save the hostage (still less the attacker) by killing the victim of the attack! If someone is threatened by a wrongful attacker, third parties have a duty to try to rescue the victim. If someone is threatened by a rightful attacker, third parties have no duty to rescue the attacked person. These obligations coincide roughly with the obligations of rescue to be found in traditional Jewish law and in the laws of Western Europe, and they are surely more intuitively appealing than any alternative solutions to the dilemmas involved. On the other hand, the notion that the right to directly defend oneself against direct attack is an absolute right coincides both with the Talmudic rule that such actions, even when directed against rightful attackers, are in some sense excusable, and are not to be punished, and with the Hobbesian notion, which is implicit in at least some Western legal systems, that no-one can really be expected not to resist death.

The right of self-defence is seen to be absolute in virtue of the nature of self-defence *as now defined*. By giving *self-defence* a narrow definition we make it possible to say that the right to *that* is absolute. We cannot reasonably infer that the (much wider) right to self-preservation is also absolute. *Self-preservation* covers a great variety of types of behaviour. Acts of individual self-preservation include taking exercise, giving up smoking, getting off heroin, buying insulin, stealing insulin from another diabetic, hoarding food, and killing innocent threats and innocent shields. At the national level it might include building defences, dismantling defences, monopolizing world food production, and killing innocent threats, for example, your enemy's children, or the people in buffer states, or your own allies if they get in the way. The right of self-preservation is limited in virtue of the large variety of possible ways of exercising that right. It would reduce all talk of rights to a nonsense if we insisted that everyone has an absolute right of self-preservation.

Since (as it seems to me) there is an absolute right of self-defence (narrowly defined) and a limited right of self-preservation (which is a wider notion) there must be situations in which it is all right for one individual to use violence on another. The difficulty, though, is to decide whether, and how, these rights are to be extended from *people* to *states*. What, for a state, is the exact equivalent of a man's right to defend himself against another man? If it can come about that the only honourable thing for a man to do is die (as soldiers sometimes must, and others too), does this mean that a national leader could ever have a duty to allow the extinction of his people? If not, can we be sure that there really is an analogy between men and states in the matter of self-defence?

Terrorism and Guerrilla War

Pacifism and the theory of the just war both draw lines between different kinds of violence and therefore each is vulnerable to the objection that violence forms a spectrum, or rather spectra, in which it is impossible to draw satisfactory lines. Thus it is argued that no lines can be drawn either in theory or in practice between aggression and defence, war and crime, the just and the unjust conduct of mass violence. Violence is a slippery slope and once you accept any you must accept all. A pacifist cannot tell in practice whether the local race riots (say) are crimes requiring 'the violence of the magistrate' or the first acts of what will turn out to be a civil war. Even in simple self-defence it might be hard to say exactly what one's actions entail. The pacifist is faced, let us say, with someone who seems to be Fletcher's Psychotic Aggressor: he responds, correctly, with a justified act of self-defence: then the Aggressor turns out to be the Archduke Ferdinand, or the American Ambassador to Iran, or some such person. Secondly, it seems that there is no clear theoretical distinction between types of violence. Terrorism, guerrilla activities, civil protests directed against government, are sometimes classified as crimes, sometimes as warfare; and some people think they are justified while others do not.

Yet is must be possible to draw lines in practice between different kinds of violence because the clergy (vocational pacifists) have been drawing such lines for themselves for centuries. The monks of Mount Athos had no qualms about repelling pirates from the mountain by force of arms in acts of self-defence but (as far as I know) they did not make themselves available for induction into the armies of nearby local potentates.[1] Or take an imaginary example: suppose a criminal lunatic breaks into a child's bedroom; suppose the child is alone in the house except for her brother who happens to be a priest. Obviously he may, indeed he must, protect his little sister, by force if need be. Is he then on a slippery slope, must he at once agree that he may, that indeed he ought, in time of war, to join the army and carry arms? No-one thinks so: the slope is not as slippery as it is alleged to be.

The slippery slope faced by the just war theorist is as follows. At the practical level, it is argued, he cannot tell whether or not the war which begins in apparent justice will be justly fought, nor can he tell in practice whether his ruler's war aims might not change with the passage of time. At the theoretical level he is faced with the dogma 'he who wills the end wills the means'. If he accepts that the aims of a war can be just, he is forced to accept the needed means; but the means *needed* might turn out to involve terrorism (say). Finally it seems that when the theory of the just war draws lines it draws them in the wrong places. Thus revolution is condemned along with terrorism for the reason that each lacks a 'proper authority'. This is counter-intuitive, for some revolutions are surely less evil than the regimes they overthrow; furthermore there is no reason why just means cannot be used in revolution if they can be used in ordinary war between states. The idea of a proper authority gets at cross purposes with other ideas about justice, creating, as it were, internal tension within the just war theory.

Nevertheless, in spite of the slippery slope arguments, seemingly ambiguous kinds of violence can in fact be distinguished from one another, at least in theory. Thus *revolutions* can be differentiated into the peaceful and the violent, so that pacifist theory can accept some but not others. *Civil protest*, similarly, can be either peaceful or violent. *Guerrilla war* is simply small war. Whether *riots* are crimes or acts of war depends on the intentions and the degree of organisation of the rioters.

The most ambigious concept in the list is that of *terrorism*, but that may be partly because it is used as a term of abuse by politicians and journalists. Yet terrorism can be defined in spite of the politicians, though even when properly defined it might turn out to remain a problem for pacifism.

Terrorism has been defined as 'the use of force or threats as a means of enforcing a political policy' and as 'the use of terror-inspiring threats as a means of governing or as a way of coercing a government or a community'. Terrorism is therefore both a method of governing, or of fighting, and a means to a specific kind of end, namely, some political end or other. Now this last seems too narrow, since certain kinds of religious persecution can surely be correctly described as terroristic, and in these days when the activities of the CIA and the Mafia and the so-called drug-barons are all muddled up together (or so we are told by the newspapers), it seems rather pedantic to say that the deeds of the first may be acts of terrorism (as political) whereas those of the second and third cannot be properly so described. On the other hand, it could be argued that the Mafia provides what is at most a border-line example of terrorism, while religious persecution can only become terroristic when it is backed up by the secular (political) arm. The word itself is not very precise, partly because it is much favoured by politicians and has been polluted by their endemic untruthfulness.

What methods of governing, or of fighting, are covered by the word *terrorism*?

A method of government which directly and with intention strikes fear into the hearts of a significant number of its own citizens by threatening them, subjecting them to arbitrary arrest, maltreating those of them it imprisons, and so on, is a reign of terror, and the world today, not to mention human history, affords enough examples.

Fighting, on the other hand, seems always likely to

inspire fear: war is by its very nature terrible and terrifying. It would seem to follow from the definitions given above that all war and all fighting is terrorism. But this is not what the word means in fact.

Is revolution the same thing as terrorism? The *OED*, in its 1950 edition, gives as examples of terrorists '(1) Jacobin under the Reign of Terror, and (2) Russian revolutionary'. Now revolution always has political or religious aims, or both, but surely when it is war it is a *type* of war, not a *method*. Its connection with terrorism, which we said *is* a method, must therefore be contingent.

Is guerrilla war the same thing as terrorism? 'Guerrilla', of course, is the diminutive of 'guerra', hence its literal meaning is 'little war'. A guerrilla soldier or fighter is one of a small band or army, and guerrilla warfare consists of skirmishes rather than battles. Thus, again, we are identifying a type of warfare rather than a method, though naturally the type in this case does to some extent dictate the methods. Obviously terrorism, unlike guerrilla activity, is not to be identified by the scale of operations: it is not a quantitative notion. Not only the style of government of Nazi Germany but also the character of the (very extensive) warfare it waged is quite correctly described as terroristic.

Let us now consider C. A. J. Coady's suggested definition of terrorism. This captures much of the current meaning of the word. Coady defines terrorism as: 'A political act, ordinarily committed by an organized group, which includes the intentional killing or other severe harming of non-combatants or the threat of the same, or intentional severe damage to the property of non-combatants or the threat of the same'.[2] Is he right about property? Suppose the PLO gave up its policies of capturing and/or threatening to kill and/or killing those civilians (of virtually any nation) which happen to fall into its hands, and instead started kidnapping very valuable works of art (again, from virtually any nation, as opportunity arose). Would this count as a change from one form of terrorism to another, or as a giving up of terrorism in favour of a different method? I think the latter: but it may be a question of degree. Works of art are not needed for life itself: the destruction of huge stores of food, or of all the buildings in a city, probably are acts of terrorism, but isn't this precisely because they cause the deaths of non-combatants? The Suffragettes took justifiable pride in the fact that during their war with the British government the only deaths were those of Suffragettes killed in prison or by suicide. The policy of the movement at one stage was to attack government property (such as post-boxes): clearly the government was a combatant. But on a few occasions private property, that is, property belonging to non-combatants, was destroyed. On Coady's account of terrorism these deeds would count as acts of terrorism, which seems counter-intuitve. It may indeed be grossly unfair and unjust to destroy the property of non-combatants, but unless that property is needed for life itself it isn't terroristic. For one thing it is not really likely to produce terror – only fury.

Is all terror political, as Coady's definition has it? For the reasons given already, it looks as if there can be non-political as well as political varieties of terrorism. That is, the ends for which the method of terrorism can be a means might sometimes be non-political. It seems right to describe some of the deeds of the Crusaders, and some of the deeds of the Mafia, as terroristic, though it may be that these are borderline cases.

In any case it is political terrorism, *qua* method of waging war, which concerns us here.

Is terrorism to be identified with all and any breach of the laws of war? And with any and every breach of the rules of the just war as traditionally understood? Coady remarks that these ways of interpreting *terrorism* involve an extension or widening of the concept. For the laws of war are as much concerned with the treatment of combatants as with the protection of civilians; and that part of the theory of the just war which has to do with *jus in bello* has injunctions about what may and may not be done to those who are captured and those who surrender – both combatants and non-combatants. But terrorism, argues Coady, is centrally, or even essentially, a matter of attacking those who ought not to be attacked, namely, non-combatants. This, he implies, is what is ordinarily understood by terrorism.

Guerrilla war, revolutionary war, and the warfare carried out by resistance movements all often involve clandestine and covert attacks. Is clandestine warfare the same thing as terrorism? Is covert war necessarily terroristic? Hidden threats may well be more terrifying than open ones, but not everything that is terrifying is terrorism, as we have already noted. On Coady's account clandestine warfare is not necessarily terroristic. Surely he is right here. Clandestine war can be directed against conventional military targets, in which case it is not terrorism. This isn't merely logically possible, it is empirically possible as well: the resistance movements in Europe during the Second World War concentrated on military targets, unlike the states engaged in that war.

Finally, since some governments are described perfectly correctly as reigns of terror, there is no reason why some wars between states should not be described as wars of terror. Terror, in short, is something that states can and do go in for. Whatever the scale of the hostilities, the label will stick if the methods involve 'the intentional killing or other severe harming of non-combatants or the threat of the same'. Thus it can be presumed that many of the acts of the CIA and of the KGB are acts of terrorism; and it is beyond question that the actual or threatened obliteration of cities is terrorism.

If terrorism is essentially a matter of attacking those who ought not to be attacked, is Coady right to identify this class with the class of non-combatants? Earlier it was argued that some border-line combatants (spies and informers) and some non-combatants (politicians, for example) are proper targets in war (if anyone is). Coady regards spies and informers as combatants. But it would be stretching the concept to include politicians.

The innocent/guilty distinction when applied to warfare generates the puzzles discussed earlier. Those puzzles are dealt with in some traditional philosophy by the invention of special new categories: involuntary guilt, unintended injustice, and the like. It would be less confusing to rest the distinction between those who *may*, and those *who ought not*, be targetted on three pairs of notions: the ordinary (un-re-defined) concepts of innocence and guilt; the concepts of combatant and non-combatant; and the distinction between self-defence and self-preservation.

Most soldiers are in somewhat the same position, morally speaking, as Fletcher's Psychotic Aggressor. That is, they know that military work involves killing, rather as the Psychotic Aggressor knows he intends to kill. Ordinary soldiers are not guilty in the way that politicians can be guilty, that is, they are not responsible for the fact that killing has started. But they are not completely innocent either (nor is the Psychotic Aggressor). In the first place, a soldier is not harmless. In the second place, he is not a mere bystander but an active participant, a professional *attacker*. Thirdly, if we think of innocence as partly a matter of someone's state of mind, we must recognize that there is always one fact that every soldier knows – that is, that he may be called upon to kill people. That is what a combatant *is*.

There are some non-combatants who are in situations which are very similar to the moral situation of a soldier. Back-benchers who vote in support of a Cabinet's decision to declare war are a possible example. Those who own or work in places where weapons are made are another. Contemporary nuclear physicists – those high priests of the scientific outlook which school children are taught to admire – are morally worse than an ordinary soldier when they are directly (and voluntarily) involved in the development or the invention of weapons of mass destruction. Furthermore, even when they are not thus directly involved, some of them must know, because everyone knows, that whenever their work can be used to refine and improve those weapons of mass destruction it will be. The French nuclear scientist who was killed in the air-raid launched by Israel against what was (allegedly) a plant for making nuclear weapons cannot be regarded as anything but a legitimate target if he really was making weapons of mass destruction to be used by Israel's enemies.

If there are types of non-combatant who count as proper targets in war, are there any *combatants* who are *not* proper targets?

What about those sheltering in a neutral country? Is it terrorism to attack a military base or operations room located inside a third country? Well, if the third country has voluntarily offered space and shelter it is not neutral anyway, whatever it might claim. Let us suppose, then, that the third country has been forced by direct military compulsion to allow the building of a base or operations room in its territory. Its neutrality has therefore been violated already: but to my mind that is not a reason to violate it again. Still, is an attack on the base a violation of this country's neutrality? In law it might not count as such: also it could be argued that the base is not any longer part of the country it lies in, but is more like an embassy – the property of the country whose military men inhabit it. Some bases do have in law an extra-territorial status. The strongest reason against attacking such a base is the danger of killing neutral civilians who live nearby. But it can be equally wrong to kill enemy civilians – enemy children for example. There is perhaps more actual danger of killing the innocent in an attack in a neutral country, since presumably there will be a higher proportion of innocent people around. But this does not answer the question as to whether the base is a legitimate target. There are practical and utilitarian reasons against attacking enemy bases located in neutral countries, or would-be neutral countries: there is the danger of widening a war; and there is the danger of antagonizing the neutral country in question. Again, these practical matters do not settle the question as to whether the kind of attack envisaged is, as such, an act of terrorism. I think the answer to the question has to be No. Soldiers target others; wherever they are, as long as they are on active service, they must expect to be targetted themselves. If they are not legitimate targets then no-one is.

What about soldiers on leave? Is it terrorism to attack a

train or a pub full of soldiers on leave? Such acts are always
described as terrorism by newspapers and politicians. Clandestine warfare is not terroristic *per se*, though one might
well feel that it is often *cowardly*. Is attacking soldiers on
leave terroristic or merely cowardly? I think it is a
borderline case, though further details might settle it one
way or another in a particular situation. I mean such
details as these: whether or not the leave was sick leave;
whether or not the soldiers were in uniform; whether or not
they were in their own country; whether or not they were
themselves being guarded by other soldiers; and so on.

Terrorism is not a matter of scale. It is not identical with
revolution; nor with guerrilla war; nor with clandestine
war. Terrorism essentially means any method of war which
consists in intentionally attacking those who ought not to
be attacked. Paradigm cases are children; the aged;
hospitals. The distinction between proper targets and
morally impermissible ones is not precisely the same as that
between the innocent and the guilty, nor is it precisely the
same as that between combatants and non-combatants.
Both pairs of notions are needed to adumbrate this
disctinction. Combatants, even the most ignorant or the
most unwilling, know that they *are* combatants, and that
they may be called upon, under discipline, to kill. They
must therefore expect to be targetted themselves. Those
responsible for starting wars, and for conscripting soldiers,
and for continuing wars, and for the general conduct of war
once started, and for making and inventing weapons, may
or may not be technically combatants. Their responsibility,
not their military or other status, makes them proper
targets. They include generals in operations rooms, politicians, spies, informers, and many scientists and tech-
nologists.

Terrorism is a style or method of government, or a style
or method of warfare.

When a government rules by terror its police forces
perpetrate deeds – such as murder and kidnapping – which
in other countries would be punished as crimes.

Terroristic warfare might be carried out by states –

obliterative war is surely terroristic – or it might be carried out by national or international political groups, with or without the open or surreptitious support of states. Not all such 'private' political military action is terroristic; for instance, D'Annunzio's capture of Fiume in 1919, whatever else was wrong with it, was not an act of *terrorism*.

The actions of a terroristic group when regarded as making up a campaign are rightly described as warfare. On the other hand, those same actions looked at individually are properly classified as civil or international crimes – that is, as arson, murder, grievous bodily harm, kidnapping, extortion, or piracy. Terrorism is sometimes treated as a series of crimes and dealt with piecemeal by police action; and at other times and in other places it is dealt with by the use of military force.

Is terrorism war or crime? It is both at once, and for that reason it poses a serious theoretical problem for pacifists. That is, there is an important question here for those pacifists (such as the Quakers) who, while rejecting war, accept 'the violence of the magistrate'. I do not think the question is unanswerable but I can only see the sketch of a possible answer myself. A pacifist might begin to develop an answer, perhaps, by pointing out that not all methods of suppressing war are themselves war. This indeed is a central tenet of Quaker or integrational pacifism. Thus, action against terrorism might be classified as necessary police work rather than as itself a species of war. Secondly, a pacifist might well remark that terrorism is only possible because rich men or rich states support it, so that it could in theory be dealt with by international negotiation and the suppression of the arms trade.

Faced with terrorism and other forms of military or quasi-military and clearly unjust violence, the pacifist and the just war theorist respond by throwing logical possibilities at one another. The pacifist says that it is *possible* to settle international disputes by non-violent methods, and the just war theorist says that it is *possible* for international violence to be used in a manner consistent with justice. Each can see that the other's possibility is no actuality.

Absolute Obligation

Although the theory of the just war and the theory of pacifism are in a sense rivals, there are some objections which can be levelled against both of them. The general objection that no lines can be drawn between different types of violence applies equally to pacifism (which in some of its forms tries to draw lines between war and personal self-defence, or between war and police action), and to the theory of the just war (which tries to draw lines, in warfare, between licit and illicit targets, intentions, aims, and leaders). This general objection (which in my view is rebuttable) rests on another objection, as follows. In attempting to draw lines, the pacifist (or the just war theorist, as the case may be) implies that there are intrinsic evils and absolute obligations: but there can be no such thing as an absolute obligation and no such thing as an action which is evil *per se*.

Is the idea of an absolute obligation ultimately incoherent? Does pacifism entail a special absolutist meta-ethic? Does the just war theory entail a special absolutist meta-ethic?

Let us begin by examining the ideas of the *intrinsic*, the *essential*, the *absolute*, and the *instrumental*.

To say that such-and-such a feature of this or that item is an intrinsic feature can mean one of several things. It can mean that the feature in question is natural rather than artificial; or that it is not merely relative; or that it is essential rather than accidental; or, in the case of a good or an evil, that it is not merely instrumental.

The ugliness of wart-hogs is not extrinsic, not external; it is not, for instance, caused by their using the wrong shade of face powder. So it is intrinsic, i.e., natural, i.e., normally found in wart-hogs. Yet it is not essential to wart-hogs that they be ugly, for it is quite conceivable that one day a wart-hog farmer might successfully breed a new and lovely variety or sub-species of this creature.

My motor-car at present has the feature of standing in a certain spatial relation R to my front door. R is an extrinsic feature which can easily change and which indeed changes constantly when the motor-car is in motion. It is unlike the car's colour which is intrinsic in the sense of being not relative, even though it too can change and hence is not essential.

It is an intrinsic, i.e., an essential feature of the series of natural numbers that it is an endless series.

In ethics *intrinsic value* contrasts with *instrumental value*. Something can have both kinds of value, of course. Philosophers have always believed, I think, that learning and knowledge, especially in the form of philosophy itself, have both intrinsic and instrumental value. *Intrinsically good* means good for its own sake, good in itself, good as an end rather than as a means. Yet to be good as an end does not mean the same as being essentially good. Because something is good, though not as a means, it does not follow that its goodness is part of its essence. The example of pleasure shows this. When pleasure is good it is good as an end – or rather, it is more usual for it to be good as an end rather than as good as a means, though it can sometimes be both. The pleasure which a normal and well-fed person takes in a delicious meal is not good as a means but as an end; the pleasure which a half-cured anorexic takes in a delicious meal is not only good in itself but also – and in this case more importantly – it is good as a means because it is likely to help the cure of the illness. Yet it is not the case that pleasure is essentially good: for it is bad to take pleasure in other people's misfortunes (say); and this must be intrinsically bad since it need have no *instrumental* effects one way or the other. Hence, pleasure can be instrumentally good or intrinsically good (or both) and it can be intrinsically bad or instrumentally bad (or both). Thus, its having intrinsic value does not entail its having essential value. (The reason is that pleasure is an intentional concept so that its value depends on that of its objects.)

Are there absolute obligations? If so, how are they generated? It is sometimes said that Utilitarianism cannot encompass the notion of an absolute obligation because it does not allow that actions may have any but instrumental worth; and the instrumental value of actions varies according to circumstances. Thus, circumstances will determine whether, for instance, one has an obligation or not to tell the truth on these or those occasions. It seems, though, that Utilitarianism is incorrect here because some actions must have intrinsic, not merely instrumental, value (or disvalue). Secondly, even if Utiltarianism were correct about this matter there would still be absolute obligations. Utlitarianism itself implies the existence of absolute obligations; the greatest happiness principle generates an absolute obligation to choose whichever action produces the greatest possible balance of pleasure over pain or happiness over unhappiness. Under that kind of description (i.e., 'productive of . . .') actions can be absolutely obligatory for Utilitarians. It seems, then, that the idea of an absolute obligation does not presuppose the idea that actions can have more than merely instrumental value. On the other hand, even though the Utilitarian assumption that actions have only instrumental value does not rule out the notion of absolute obligation, it does rather suggest that the content of that notion is somewhat minimal.

However, it seems that at least some actions must have intrinsic value, or rather disvalue. Killing people must be a counter-example to the generalization that actions have only instrumental value, and if there can be one counter-example there are probably others. Killing is by definition an action which is followed by a state of affairs in which the victim no longer exists. Now Smith's non-existence is not necessarily an evil state of affairs. If Smith was born in 1905 and died a natural death in 1985 it follows that he did not exist in 1904 and will not exist in 1999; but these facts are not *evils*. Secondly, when he no longer exists he cannot suffer pleasure and pain and therefore cannot be a subject of Utilitarian calculations. How then can killing him be *instrumentally* bad? Yet surely it is *bad*; virtually all men fear death and virtually all men would regard the prospect of being murdered as a specially bad way to die. It seems then that killing, the action, is intrinsically evil if it is evil.

Do intrinsic goods and evils generate absolute obligations; and is it from intrinsic goods and evils that absolute obligations (if any) arise? If so, do all intrinsic goods and evils generate absolute obligations; and are all such obligations generated only by intrinsic goods or evils? It seems that the intrinsically good is neither necessary nor sufficient for the generation of an absolute obligation. Firstly, because some actions which are aimed at the intrinsically good are self-regarding or prudential, and it is not certain that one can have obligations – let alone absolute obligations – towards oneself. Secondly, some intrinsic goods form parts of wholes which are overall less intrinsically good than other intrinsically good wholes. Thirdly, to be intrinsically good does not mean the same thing as being importantly good. *Intrinsic* only means here *non-instrumental*; there is no reason why an intrinsic good cannot be trivial. This must, in fact, be the case with many small pleasures; similarly, pain is intrinsically rather than instrumentally evil, but a slight headache is a very trivial evil. It is contrary to common sense to suppose that every intrinsic good (or evil) generates an obligation, let alone an absolute obligation. Fourthly, one sometimes has to choose between two or more apparently equal goods. Thus, it seems that there could not be an absolute obligation to choose one rather than the other, though there may perhaps be an obligation to choose at least one such good, an obligation not to behave like Buridan's ass.

Obviously there can be no obligation to choose a lesser

rather than a greater good. When there are two equal but incompatible goods to choose between, there is no obligation to choose one rather than the other. In choosing between unequal goods 'I chose the lesser good' is a confession of having acted wrongly or imprudently (with or without an excuse), whereas the claim 'I chose the greater good' is, if true, a completely adequate justification of what one has done. But since it seems to be logically possible that one might have to choose between equal goods, it follows that there can be no absolute obligation generated merely by the fact that a good is an intrinsic good, even an important intrinsic good.

An absolute obligation, if there are any, is one that must be carried out, come what may. Now this notion is much less problematic if we consider the avoiding of evil deeds rather than the performing of good ones. For in the latter case there will always be difficult questions about *when* and *where*. Given that I have an obligation to perform some good deed, does it matter when I perform it? Is it all right to postpone performance, and if so, for how long? What are the rules here? If once I have decided to perform my good deed, must I keep on performing it perpetually, or what? There are no very clear answers to these questions. But in the case of refraining from evil there is no problem: the answer to the question 'When and where must I refrain from evil deeds?' is quite clear, it is 'always and everywhere'. Secondly, the most familiar and telling examples of absolute obligation are negative, things one must not do rather than things one ought to do. According to traditional Jewish law, for instance, there are actions which a proper Jew is not permitted to do under any circumstances; ideally a Jew will choose his own death rather than commit idolatory, or murder, or incest. Somewhat similarly, Thomist philosophy teaches that divine law, and much natural law, must be obeyed come what may: Catholic teaching on abortion is a good illustration. Secular thinking, too, allows for the existence of absolute obligation (whatever secular philosophy says): for instance, under military law a soldier is not permitted to run away from battle in defiance of orders; according to at least some ways of thinking a soldier is, *par excellence*, a man who must die rather than perform certain deeds.

Do intrinsic evils generate absolute obligations? A trivial evil, like a trivial good, does not necessarily generate obligation, still less absolute obligation. An evil suffered only by oneself cannot generate obligation unless one can have obligations towards oneself.

What are we to say about choosing between evils? Choosing between evils is different from choosing between goods. In choosing between unequal evils 'I chose the greater evil' is, of course, a confession of having acted wrongly (with or without an excuse). But unlike 'I chose the greater good', 'I chose the lesser evil' is not a justification but an excuse. And 'I was faced with a forced choice between two equal evils' is also an excuse as well as an explanation. Thus in these two kinds of case it is presupposed that there is something bad about one's actions that needs excusing. In choosing between goods, excuses are only in order if one has chosen the lesser good, and when goods are equal there is no wrong choice. But in choosing between evils one feels one has to make excuses not only for the wrong decision (i.e., for choosing the greater evil) but also for the right one (i.e., for choosing the lesser evil).

Another apparent difference between good and evil deeds is as follows. For any type of intrinsically good deed one can think of, it is conceivable that in some circumstances it will turn out to be impossible to perform both of two such deeds; hence there can be no obligation (and *ergo* no absolute obligation) to perform both, and when one chooses one rather than the other one does not thereby fail in one's obligations. For there cannot be an obligation to do what is impossible. On the other hand, however, there seems no reason why one could not *refrain* from any number of evil actions simultaneously. There is surely no difficulty in refraining from 100 things at once. Now, if this is true, it is always possible to carry out all one's absolute obligations, provided that they are negative, i.e., obligations to refrain from doing things. Secondly, as already noted, the most convincing examples of absolute obligation are prohibitions. Thus, for various reasons, it seems likely that if there are any absolute obligations they are generated by intrinsic evil rather than by intrinsic good.

Well, is there any reason in principle why intrinsic evils could not generate absolute obligations?

Some refrainings are very naturally described also as performances. Thus refraining from breaking a promise is the same thing as carrying out the promised action. Some people would claim, further, that *refusing* (for instance, to serve in a war, or to kill civilians) is a positive action and not a mere refraining. I do not think it is safe to generalize, to conclude that *all* refrainings arc perfomances under a different name; however, not all anti-absolutist arguments require this generalization. The central anti-absolutist assertion here is that – either because refrainings are really performings, or for some other reason – one can be faced with choices betwen refrainings from evils just as one can be faced with choices between good deeds. For any evil deed you can think of, you can conceive either a situation in which it would be wrong not to do that deed, or one in which it would be somehow impossible not to do it. The proof of this assertion consists in examples. Thus Agamemnon was forced to choose between not killing Iphigenia and not breaking a promise to the gods; Anna Karenina had to choose between deserting her young son and giving up her lover; Gauguin (or, rather, the fictitious character Strickland) had to choose between abandoning his wife and abandoning his art; the man on the runaway trolley has to choose between steering it into the left-hand track (where it will kill x people) and steering it into the right-hand track (where it will kill y people).[1]

It seems, though, that the examples produced by anti-absolutists are feeble. Some are not examples of obligation and some are not examples of forced choice (though alleged to be such). Agamemnon's supposedly forced choice between disobeying the gods and destroying his daughter, although in some sense a real conflict, was surely not a conflict between real obligations, it was a conflict between what he *took* to be his obligations – which is a very different matter. Anna Karenina's choice between her lover and her son is not a conflict between two obligations; it is, rather, a conflict between a very important but possibly not an absolute obligation (to the son), and an excusable or conceivably even a justifiable wish to escape from an unhappy marriage into an apparently happier life. The real Gauguin's separation from his wife was not in the circumstances an abrogation of either financial or emotional responsibility, and hence any conflict in the situation was not one involving an obligation to her: nor was his travelling to the South Seas a carrying out of an obligation to himself. Strickland's conflict, in Somerset Maugham's novel *The Moon and Sixpence*, loosely based on Gauguin's life, is not a conflict between obligations but a conflict between art and (conventional) morality. No-one has an *obligation* to be an artist. It would be interesting if philosophical moralists were to seriously weigh up the real Gauguin's good and bad behaviour – his devotion to his art versus his dreadful (and racist) treatment of all the Pacific Islanders whom he knowingly infected with venereal disease; but it would not necessarily prove that there are there no absolute obligations. The runaway trolley cases are not cases of choosing between evil deeds but of choosing under constraint of circumstances between evil outcomes. The trolley-rider is *ex hypothesi* only marginally responsible (if at all) for those circumstances; the example, therefore, is not relevant to questions about obligation.

To some philosophers evils are like numbers – you can always imagine a bigger one. You might think you have an absolute obligation to avoid doing the evil deed E1, but what do you do if the alternative is to perform a worse deed, E2? There can be no final, absolute, obligation to refrain from E1, nor from E2 (because E3 may be worse), nor from E3 (since E4 may be worse) . . . etc. The number series itself might be used to make the point. The worse evil (E2, say) is represented not as a different evil from E1 but as a multiplication of it. It is asked: 'If killing one person is bad, surely killing two is worse? And killing three worse than killing two? For surely killing $n + 1$ is worse than killing n! So there is no absolute obligation to refrain from killing one person . . . or two . . . or three . . . or n'. But the numbers game argument is too powerful. Its real conclusion is that there need be no obligation to refrain from killing any number of people, short of an infinite number. It simultaneously uses, and undermines, the notion of obligation, and ultimately leaves no way of making decisions at all.

The strongest argument against absolute obligation stems not from the supposed possibility of forced choices between oneself performing one of two equally evil deeds but from the possibility of choices between performing an evil deed oneself and failing to prevent someone else from doing something bad or dangerous. There is no general obligation to prevent everyone else's bad deeds, but some jobs involve this as a duty (policeman, mental nurse, security guard). Situations of self-preservation (as defined earlier) and of rescue may well present choices between doing something evil oneself, and allowing another to.

Which obligations are absolute, and which are defeasible? Not every intrinsic good or evil generates absolute obligation: how can we know which ones do? Well, it might be suggested that what we need is the idea of the *essentially bad* (or good) which, as we have seen, is not the same as the intrinsically bad (or good). But not even essentially bad states of affairs can generate absolute obligation. Pain is essentially bad – that is, it would not be pain if it were not bad – but there is no obligation to refrain from causing pain *come what may*: dentists sometimes have to cause pain. As to actions, the notion of an *essentially* bad action must surely be exactly the same as the notion of one which has an absolute obligation to refrain from: it cannot be used to help us understand that idea.

The Catholic doctrine of double effect, which teaches that it can be licit to bring about as an unintended but foreseen side-effect which it would be illicit to bring about intentionally, is one way of dealing with the problems surrounding the idea of absolute obligation. The doctrine, though, does not seem to be wholly consistent with the idea of an obligation to refrain from certain deeds *come what may*. Similarly, and more obviously, the Catholic teaching on dispensation from the law is not wholly consistent with *this* notion of absolute obligation.

It seems to me that there is more reason to believe that there are absolute obligations than that there are not: more reason, on balance, to suppose that there are kinds of deeds which no decent person could choose to do, come what may. But do pacifists and just war theorists have to believe this? Pacifism and the theory of the just war both come to us from Christianity and hence it is probable that most of their adherents have, in fact, believed in absolute obligation. But the doctrines do not themselves entail the existence of absolute obligation. It is of the nature of philosophical theories about morality that they should explain and be consistent with most ordinary moral codes. It is in the nature of moral codes that, in general, each of them is susceptible of more than one kind of philosophical explanation. All moral codes draw lines between the licit and the impermissible, but no philosopher has ever objected that in doing this vegetarianism (say), or monogamism, or anti-racism, or militarism, simply *has to* accept an absolutist meta-ethic. Why are pacifism and the just war theory picked out in this way? Pacifism involves conflict between the individual and his government: so too does the just war theory if it is stripped of the inessential premise that the prince, not the subject, must decide what is just. It is as if the philosophers thought that only an ethical absolutist could have the right to stand up to the all-powerful state. But that is by no means self-evidently true.

War-resisters do not all hold exactly the same opinions about the morality of war. Some believe that war is evil because violence is evil, some think that war is evil because killing human beings is evil, some believe that war is evil because large-scale killing of human beings is evil, some think war is evil because it necessarily involves the evil of killing innocent civilians.

A principled person can become 'anti-this' or 'anti-that' not so much because of what 'this' or 'that' is in theory, but because of what 'this' or 'that' is, or must be, in practice. Thus in the 1930s a man might have been anti-German because of what the German nation had become in fact. People are anti-Communist, often, not on account of anything written by Marx or Engels but rather because of what Communist states are like in real life: they might argue, too, that what Communism is like in real life is no accident but is what it *must* be like in spite of what is *logically* possible. Anti-Catholicism, I guess, is more often brought on by the bad and worldly behaviour of Catholic institutions than by thoughts about the truth or otherwise of religious doctrine. Many people are anti-war simply because of what war, with the help of scientists, has become.

Philosophers continue to insist that war could, logically, be all right, ignoring the powerful reasons which make the logical possibility of a just war a non-actuality. To suggest that these reasons are merely a matter of human wickedness is to simplify the problem and caricature the difficulties. Generals and politicians, whatever they might say in speeches, show in their practice that they do not think that just methods are liable to succeed in achieving the aim of war, which is victory; and perhaps if philosophers become generals or politicians they might come to agree with that judgement.

War as a state of affairs is evil in part because of its results. In this it is like earthquakes and tornadoes, only worse. Also it is, *of course*, evil intrinsically and essentially. In this is resembles cancer and leprosy and syphilis, except that it is worse. Anyone who says that war *per se* is not intrinsically evil, that it may sometimes even be 'sacred' or 'holy', must be off his head. One might as well say that brain tumours are sacred. War is *obviously* intrinsically and essentially evil. War by definition entails killing and death and wounds and mutilations of all kinds. War necessarily involves injustice on at least one side, and more usually there is injustice on both sides. War always involves the suffering and destruction of innocent people, on any definition of innocence that you care to opt for, either because they are deliberately targetted, or as a 'mere' side-effect. Anyone who instigates war between his neighbours or who embarks on aggressive or defensive war knows, if he stops to think, that these effects and side-effects are inevitable. We can add that even from a Utilitarian standpoint it is clear that war is the worst possible way of resolving differences. Finally, war is a test of might and is therefore inherently incapable of settling questions of right.

It is, I daresay, extremely rare for someone to be faced with a forced choice between leprosy and cancer (say), indeed I suspect that such a choice is not logically possible – though perhaps some philosophical machine somewhere has constructed an appropriate 'scenario'. On the other hand, it is possible for a national leader to be faced with a forced choice between the two specific intrinsic evils of engaging in a defensive war and allowing some dreadful catastrophe such as genocide to overwhelm his people. It seems to me that, faced with *that* forced choice between evils, a national leader ought to opt for the former if the people are capable of putting up a fight. It cannot be emphasized too much, though, that nearly all national leaders who embark on war, or who decide to develop or use cruel and abominable methods of warfare, will claim that their choices were forced. Truman suggested strongly that he was *forced* to choose to 'save [combatant] American lives' by obliterating large numbers of Japanese non-combatants. Leaders will even claim that they are *forced* by the other side, or by purely economic factors, to develop napalm, mustard gas, bacterial weapons, and nuclear missiles. Hitler seems to have alleged that sheer impatience with the international situation *forced* him to march into most of the countries of Europe.

Suppose a weak nation is faced with a forced choice between undergoing genocide and defending itself with cruel and indiscriminate methods of warfare, these happening to be the only ones available. Human beings have brought about the extinction of several other animal species, usually by accident or through a kind of negligence:

they have also wiped out some of the races of humanity itself, *on purpose*, for example, in Tasmania, the Caribbean, and South America. Now imagine that the Tasmanians, a weak and primitive people armed only with weapons made of wood, had chanced upon a substance containing bacteria which caused a fatal, very painful, and highly infectious disease to which they themselves were immune. Having discovered (as in real life they did discover) that the British settlers on the island intended to hunt them down like animals and exterminate their race, would they have been justified in choosing to throw the infectious substance into the homes of the settlers, knowing that it would cause the painful deaths not only of the menfolk with the guns, but also of babes in arms and other innocents? It is a fault in the theory of the just war that while it (rightly in my view) answers Yes to this question, it answers Yes for wrong reasons, namely, for reasons which will also allow men in situations of *unforced* choice to use weapons which kill the innocent – possibly in huge numbers. These reasons are the thesis that it can be all right, not only in situations of forced choice between terrible evils such as genocide, but also elsewhere, to kill innocent people *as a side-effect*; and the thesis that, having embarked on a just war, one may do *whatever is judged essential to win*; which, of course, might easily include unjust means.

Although the doctrines of pacifism and the theory of the just war are in a sense rivals, it is not possible to decide that one is true and the other is false. This is for two reasons. The first reason, which is relatively unimportant, is that both pacifism and the theory of the just war take different forms. There is more than one kind of pacifism, and there are varieties of just war theory. The second reason is fundamental: it is this. Those pacifists who say that war is intrinsically and essentially evil, and different, therefore, from certain other kinds of violence, are surely right. But they are mistaken (in my view) if they infer from that, that there are absolutely no situations, real or imaginary, in which taking up arms could be the lesser intrinsic evil in a forced choice. On the other hand, those who adhere to a more or less traditional version of the theory of the just war, are (in my view) right to say that fighting might sometimes be the lesser evil – at least in imaginary situations. But they are mistaken if they infer from this that it can be all right to choose war when there is no *forced* choice; or that choosing war can be good (rather than excusable); or that war *per se* is not intrinsically evil; or that, given that the cause is just, any means which are essential for victory are all right. That last proposition is a piece of (infernal) machinery for making all wars seem just.

We might well say that the point is not to justify war but to abolish it. The pacifist by his actions in war and peace at least proves that he really believes *that*.

Appendix 1

Philosophers and Others on War

Buddhist precepts (for monks):

A Bhikkhu who kills a human being with his own hands or by his instructions or at his instigation or who is an accessory to the killing . . . is said to commit a Parajika sin [a 'mortal' sin]. . . .

If a Bhikkhu goes to see any large organised body of men armed for war, he is said to commit a Prayascitta sin [a 'venial' sin] unless he has sufficient reason for his act. . . .

If a Bhikkhu finds it necessary to go to the army [e.g., to visit a sick relative] he should not remain for more than three days. . . .

When a Bhikkhu remains with an army for three days, he is not allowed to go to the battle-field, a soldiers' camp, or a temporary encampment where the troops mounted on horses, on elephants, on chariots, and the infantry troops are concentrated to fight a battle. . . .

(Bhikkhu Yen-Kiat, *Mahayana Vinaya* (Bangkok 1960)

Tertullian:

We must 'render unto Caesar the things that are Caesar's' – happily he added: 'And to God the things that are God's'. What then is Caesar's? Surely the subject of the original discussion, whether or not tribute should be paid to Caesar. That is why the Lord asked to see a coin and asked whose image it bore. When he heard that it was Caesar's, he said 'Render to Caesar the things that are Caesar's, and unto God the things that are God's', that is, render to Caesar Caesar's image, which is on the coin, and to God God's image, which is man. To Caesar then you should render money, to God yourself. If everything belongs to Caesar what will be God's?

. . . It is being asked whether a baptized Christian can turn to military service and whether a soldier may be admitted to the faith, at least the rank and file who are not compelled to offer sacrifices or impose capital sentences. There is no compatibility between the oath to serve God and the oath to serve man, between the standard of Christ and the standard of the devil, the camp of light and the camp of darkness. One life cannot be owed to two masters, God and Caesar. Of course – if you like to make a jest of the subject – Moses carried a rod and Aaron wore a buckle, John had a leather belt, Joshua led an army and Peter made war. Yes, but tell me how he will make war, indeed how he will serve in peacetime, without a sword – which the Lord took away? Even if the soldiers came to John and were given instructions to keep, even if the centurion believed, the Lord afterwards unbelted every soldier when he disarmed Peter.

(*On Idolatry*)

Origen:

We should also say this to those who are alien to our faith and ask us to fight for the community and to kill men: that it is your opinion that the priests of certain images and wardens of the temples of the gods, as you think them to be, should keep their right hand undefiled for the sake of sacrifices, that they may offer the customary sacrifices to those who you say are gods with hands unstained by blood and pure from murders. And in fact when war comes to you do not enlist priests. If, then, this is reasonable, how much more reasonable is it that, while others fight, Christians also should be fighting as priests and worshippers of God, keeping their right hands pure.

(*Contra Celsum*)

Augustine:

What is the evil of war? Is it the death of some who will soon die in any case, that others may live in peaceful subjection? This is mere cowardice, not any religious feeling. The real evils in war are love of violence, revengeful cruelty, fierce and implacable enmity, wild resistance, and the lust for power, and such like; and it is to punish these things, when force is needed to inflict the punishment, that, in obedience to God or some lawful authority, good men undertake wars . . . the Lord Jesus Christ himself ordered tribute money to be given to Caesar . . . for tribute money is given for the purpose of paying soldiers for war . . . Since a righteous man, serving, it may be, under an unrighteous king, may do the duty belonging to his position in the State by fighting on the order of his king – for in some cases it is plainly the will of God that he should fight, and in others, where this is not plain, the soldier is innocent because his position makes obedience a duty – how much more must the man be blameless who carries on war on the authority of God? . . . "Resist not evil" (means) not a bodily action but an inward disposition.

(*Contra Faustum*)

The Lollards' Petition:

. . . manslaughter by battle or pretended law of justice for temporal cause or spiritual, without special revelation, is expressly contrary to the New Testament, which is a law full of grace and mercy. This conclusion is openly proved by the example of Christ preaching here on earth, who taught us to love and have mercy on our enemies and not to kill them.

(English Historical Documents IV, p. 849.)

The miller John Skilly confesses to heresy:

'Also I held, taught and affirmed that relics of saints that is to say flesh or bone of any dead man should not be worshipped by the people nor enshrined. Also I held, taught and affirmed that it is not lawful for any man to fight or do battle for a realm or a country, or to go to law for any right or wrong.'

(English Historical Documents IV, p. 865)

Francisco Suarez:

The first heresy [in connection with war] is the assertion that it is intrinsically evil and contrary to charity to wage war. Such is the heretical belief attributed by Augustine to the Manicheans, whom Wycliffe followed, according to the testimony of Waldensis. The second error is the assertion that war is specifically forbidden to Christians, and, especially, war against Christians . . . persons of our own time, who are heretics, advance (this) contention.

Our first conclusion is that war, absolutely speaking, is not intrinsically evil, nor is it forbidden to Christians . . . this is a matter of faith.

War is not opposed to the love of one's enemies; for whoever wages war honourably hates, not individuals, but the actions which he justly punishes.

Even when war is aggressive, it is not an evil in itself, but may be right and necessary. The fact is evidenced by the custom of the Church, one that has quite frequently been approved by the Fathers and the Popes . . . in this connection, we may also refer to (the opinion of) Torquemada . . . aggressive war is often necessary to the state, in order to ward off acts of injustice and hold enemies in check.

In order that a war may be justly waged, a number of conditions must be observed. . . . First, the war must be waged by a legitimate power; secondly, the cause itself and the reason must be just; thirdly, the method of its conduct must be proper.

I hold that the sovereign ruler is bound to make a diligent examination of the cause and its justice and that after making this examination he ought to act in accordance with the knowledge thus obtained. I hold that generals and other chief men in the kingdom, whenever they are summoned for consultation to give their opinion, are bound to inquire diligently into the truth of the matter; but if they are not called, they are under no greater obligation than common soldiers. I hold that common soldiers, as subjects of princes, are in no wise bound to make diligent investigation, but rather may go to war when ordered to do so, provided it is not clear to them that the war is unjust . . . subjects when in doubt are bound to obey their superiors . . . nor do I find any difference between subjects and non-subjects [i.e., mercenaries].

(*A Work on the Theological Virtues*)

Kant:

There used to be an inn in Holland with the sign of "Perpetual Peace", and on the signboard was depicted a graveyard. Whether the satire was aimed at all mankind, or only at the rulers of states, or, may be, only at philosophers who dream this sweet dream, is a question that may here be left unanswered. . . .

Just as we despise savages for their attachment to their lawless liberty, and for their preference for perpetual fighting among themselves rather than for submission to a legitimate constraint to be established by themselves, i.e., for licence rather than for reasonable liberty, regarding this with deep contempt and stigmatising it as brutal, uncouth and a bestial degradation of humanity, in just the same way, one might imagine, civilised nations (each constituting an independent state) should hasten to escape from such a villainous condition the sooner the better. Instead of this every State sets its majesty (for the majesty of a people is an inconsistent term) just in this, to be subject to no external legitimate constraint, and the glory of its ruler consists in having many thousands at his command to let themselves be sacrificed for an affair that does not concern them, without himself needing to run the slightest risk.

The difference between European and American savages lies chiefly in this – that while many tribes of the latter have been entirely consumed by their enemies, the former know of a better method of utilising their conquered enemies than to eat them, preferring to increase the number of their subjects and consequently of their tools for even more widespread wars.

Considering the wickedness of human nature, which can be seen undisguised in the free relationship between peoples (though well masked through the constraint of government inside the legalised civic State), it is very curious that it has not yet been possible wholly to expunge the word justice from the politics of war as being pedantic ... (the) verbal homage that every State pays to the moral law proves that there is a greater moral disposition to be found in mankind, though dormant at present, some day in spite of all to master his evil genius (whose existence he cannot deny) and to hope the same of others. For otherwise the word justice would never be uttered by States that wish to fight each other except in mockery.

(*Perpetual Peace*)

Appendix 2

Deterrent Threats

It has recently been argued that, although it would be act of criminal terrorism to launch a nuclear missile at a city, there is nothing wrong with merely threatening to do that. The reasons given are various. One reason given is that intentions as such are not punishable in law and hence cannot be evil or good, right or wrong. Intentions are mere thoughts and thoughts as such are morally neutral unless they issue in action.

However, in the first place, intentions are not mere thoughts: it is of their nature to be expressed in preparations; in the case supposed, in preparations to obliterate large numbers of people. Secondly, all our moral thinking allows that intentions can be of good or evil: hence being good or evil must be a different matter from being punishable or rewardable. For if someone spontaneously gives up an intention to do what it would be evil to do this counts as a moral improvement in him. Again, intentions to do what it would be evil to do are perceived as themselves evil for the further reason that an intention to do a deed increases the likelihood that you will do it from a notional zero to some real probability. It would not *be* an intention if that were not the case. A categorical intention raises the probability *simpliciter*; but it is alleged that a merely conditional intention might not raise the likelihood (of your doing the deed) at all. For, it is said, provided that the conditional intention is *expressed* it operates as a threat or a warning, and the purpose of a threat or a warning is to remove the condition under which you *would* do the deed. Thus, the expression of a conditional intention may well make it less likely that you will do the deed which you conditionally intend to do, than would be the case if you remained silent on the matter. But that, of course, says nothing about what effect simply *holding* conditional intentions has on the probability of your doing the deed. Simply *holding* a conditional intention surely raises the probability of doing the deed, even if it does not raise the probability as much as holding a categorical intention obviously must. Thus it cannot be argued that having intentions is morally neutral. For although it was agreed that expressing a conditional intention, or threat, might reduce the probability of your carrying out the deed, this is only a reduction relative to what would happen if you kept silent about your intention; not one relative to what would happen if you never had it in the first place. In the real world open threats are not favoured by military men and it is part of nuclear strategy to keep one's intentions fairly secret, *contra* the arguments of philosophers who try to justify the theory of deterrence.

Holding a conditional intention (as against not having the intention in the first place) increases the empirical probability that you will from time to time alter your conditions. Certainly this has happened in the case of the nuclear threat. In the real world the announced conditions for launching nuclear weapons have not remained static, not have the (announced) reasons for owning them in the first place. The original reason given by politicians for building arsenals of nuclear weapons was financial; in the 1940s and 1950s it was said that these weapons would be less costly than standing armies, and figures were produced to prove it. At that time, too, the condition stated by the West for launching a nuclear attack was a conventional land invasion into Europe by Russia: a policy of nuclear first strike, in fact. Unfortunately ordinary citizens have no way of knowing when or how the conditions under which their government or its allies would launch a nuclear war might change in the future and no say in deciding directly on those possible conditions. Nor, in the prevailing conditions of secrecy, can they know whether the stated intentions, conditional or otherwise, of their governments are genuine or bluff or what.

If we can assume that intentions as such can be good or evil, what makes them so? Surely their content: what else could be relevant? But this has in fact been challenged by some, who argue that only a categorical intention to do what is evil could be evil itself. An expressed conditional intention is a threat, and its purpose is to prevent an enemy from doing something evil to you. If it works it prevents evil, and is therefore good.

However, exactly the same thing could be said of a categorical intention which frightened the enemy into such fits that he could not attack, and which then, for some reason or other, was not carried out. The idea that there is a moral difference between categorical intentions and conditional intentions rests on and needs *both* Utilitarianism *and* the mistaken premise that if an intention is categorical it will, in fact, be carried out. Consider a man who forms a conditional intention to murder his stepchild unless the neighbours turn off their radio. They do, so he doesn't. Compare him with a man who forms a categorical intention to murder his stepchild come what may, but who is prevented from carrying out his intention by the intervention of the NSPCC. Surely there can be no moral difference between these two men, or between these two intentions. Is this because of the triviality of the condition of the conditional intention? Well then, imagine that the first man forms a conditional intention to murder his stepchild unless the neighbours don't stop torturing their lodger, or stockpiling petrol bombs, or throwing hand-grenades in the street. Suppose for some reason this threat worked. Are we to infer from this kind of case the principle that a threat to do what it would be evil to do is not itself evil provided only that the condition itself is evil and the threat works? The inference does not seem apodeictic, to say the least, and in fact there are three reasons for rejecting the conclusion. Two have already been mentioned; these are: one, in real life everyone counts the giving up of an intention to do what it would be evil to do as a sign of moral improvement; two, the sheer fact of forming an intention to do an evil deed increases the probability that you will do it. This raising of the probability, is, as it were, prior to the *expression* of the intention, which may indeed then lower the probability, whether or not the intention was conditional. The third reason for rejecting the proposed principle is that if it were true it would be impossible to know whether your own or anyone else's intentions were good or bad until after the success or the failure of the threats they are expressed in. On this principle when the first (post-Nagasaki) act of obliterative war takes place we will know for the first time that the conditional intentions embodied in the Great Powers' policies of deterrence are evil, for at that point they will *become* evil, retrospectively presumably. But if no such act ever takes place (ever?) then at some moment of time (when?) we will find out that the conditional intentions to do something it would be evil to do were not themselves evil. This consideration is a particular application of a fundamental objection to Utilitarianism, namely that by the time you know an action is right or wrong it will be too late for your knowledge to affect your conduct. (In real life it seems likely that, if and when the first (post-Nagasaki) act of obliterative war takes place, those who have argued for a Utilitarian view of intentions will not in fact deduce that the intention to obliterate has turned out to be evil after all, but will revert to a non-Utilitarian account which will allow them to argue that the politicians were unlucky but well-meaning.)

The continuing conditional intention to wage obliterative war has affected the way nations think about each other. At the beginning of the Cold War, politicians still used to say piously 'We do not hate the enemy people, only their wicked system of government'. It is a long time since any politician said that, the words must be sticking in their throats.

Is an evil intention just as bad as an evil deed? Of course not. For one thing, you can give up the intention but you cannot undo the deed. But it doesn't follow that the intention must be all right after all, nor does it follow that it is a lesser evil which you ought to opt for. There cannot be a forced choice between an intention and the thing it intends! Finally, there is no self-contradiction in supposing that two things may be unequally evil and yet both be beyond the pale. This is how it is with obliteration and the conditional intention to obliterate.

Notes

Chapter 1: The Meaning of Pacifism

1 G. B. Shaw, *Prefaces* (London 1934), p. 382.
2 Peter Brock, *Pacifism in Europe to 1914* (Princeton 1972), p. 472 f.
3 John Yoder, *Nevertheless* (Pennsylvania 1971), *passim*.

Chapter 2: The Origins of Pacifism

1 Brock, *Pacifism in Europe*, p. 3
2 Tertullian, *On Idolatry* (Ante-Nicene Christian Library, *Tertullian*, Edinburgh 1869), ch. XIX, p. 171.
3 Origen, *Contra Celsum*, trans. Henry Chadwick (Cambridge 1953), p. 509 f.
4 Brock, *Pacifism in Europe*, p. 14.
5 David C. Douglas (ed.), *English Historical Documents IV* (Cambridge 1969), p. 849.
6 *New Catholic Encyclopedia*, vol. 14 (Washington, D.C. 1967), p. 804.
7 Austin Flannery (ed.), *Vatican Council II* (Dublin 1974), pp. 988–91.
8 Pius XII, cited in *New Catholic Encyclopedia*, vol. 14 (Washington, D.C. 1967), p. 804.
9 National Conference of Catholic Bishops (of the USA), *The Challenge of Peace: a Pastoral Letter on War and Peace* (Chicago 1983), p. 25.

10 John XXIII (1963), *Pacem in Terris* (Catholic Truth Society pamphlet, London).

Chapter 3: Pacifism and Conscription

1 G. E. M. Anscombe, 'War and Murder', *Collected Papers III* (Oxford 1981), p. 55.
2 *Encyclopaedia Britannica*, 'War'.
3 Brock, *Pacifism in Europe*, chs 1–6, *passim*.
4 Brock, *Pacifism in Europe*, p. 478; *Pacifism in the United States* (Princeton 1968), p. 903 f. See also his *Twentieth Century Pacifism* (New York 1973), *passim*.

Chapter 4: Violence and Contradiction

1 See, e.g., Peter Singer, *Animal Liberation* (London 1976), *passim*.
2 See, e.g., Newton Garver, 'What Violence Is' in James Rachels and Frank A. Tilman (eds), *Philosophical Issues – a Contemporary Introduction* (New York 1972); R. P. Wolff, 'On Violence', *Journal of Philosophy* 66, 1969; J.Schaffer (ed.), *Violence* (New York 1971).
3 Jan Narveson, 'Pacifism, a Philosophical Analysis', in R. A. Wasserstrom (ed.), *War and Morality* (California 1970).

Chapter 5: The Violence of the State

1 Augustine, *On the Sermon on the Mount* (Library of the Nicene and Post-Nicene Fathers vi, Grand Rapids 1887), pp. 24–31; *Contra Faustum* (*The Works of St Augustine* vol. v, Edinburgh 1872), p. 463 f.
2 Francisco Vitorio, *De Indis et de jure belli relectiones*, ed. E. Nys, trans. J. P. Bate (Washington 1917), editor's Introduction, p. 63.
3 Ibid., pp. 166 and 171.
4 Romans 13.

5 John Calvin, *Institutions of the Christian Church*, trans. F. L. Battles (London 1961), Book IV, Ch. XX, *passim*.
6 G. E. M Anscombe, 'War and Murder', *Collected Papers III* (Oxford 1981), p. 55, p. 57.

Chapter 6: The Just War

1 Anon., *The Song of Roland*, trans. C. K. Scott-Moncrieff (Ann Arbor 1959), LXXXIX, CXIX, CXXVI.
2 F. H. Russell, *The Just War in the Middle Ages* (Cambridge 1975), pp. 73–4.
3 H. E. J. Cowdrey, 'The Peace of God', *Past and Present* 46, 1970, pp. 42–67.
4 H. E. J. Cowdrey, 'Bishop Ermenfried of Sion and the Penitential Ordinance following the Battle of Hastings', *Journal of Ecclesiastical History* 20, 1969.
5 Russell, *Just War*, pp. 35–6, 39, 59, 75.
6 Ibid., pp. 145–6
7 Thomas Hobbes, *Leviathan* (Penguin Books, London 1968), chs 14 and 15, *passim*.
8 Aquinas, *Summa Theologica* (Blackfriars and Eyre & Spottiswoode, London 1966) (vols 38 and 47), 2a2e, Q. 64, Q. 188.
9 Russell, *Just War*, p. 277.
10 Francisco Vitorio, *De Indis et de jure belli relectiones*, ed. E. Nys, trans. J. P. Bate (Washington 1917), editor's Introduction, p. 63.
11 Ibid., *passim*.
12 Hugo Grotius, *The Law of War and Peace*, trans. F. W. Kelsey (Oxford 1825).

Chapter 7: Guilt and Innocence

1 G. E. M. Anscombe, 'War and Murder', *Collected Papers III* (Oxford 1981), p. 53
2 Nicholas Denyer, 'Just War', in Hide Ishiguro (ed.), *The Philosophy of G. E.M. Anscombe* (The Hague – forthcoming).

3 A. Roberts and R. Guellf (eds), *Documents on the Laws of War* (Oxford 1982), pp. 155 f.; pp. 430 f.

Chapter 8: Self-Defence

1 'Criminal Law', in Menachem Elon (ed.), *The Principles of Jewish Law* (Jerusalem 1975), pp. 470 f.
2 Judith Jarvis Thomson, 'Self-defense and rights', Findley Lecture (Kansas University 1976), pp. 3 and 10.
3 George P. Fletcher, 'The right to life', *Monist* 63, 1980.
4 According to Havelock Ellis: see his *The Psychology of Sex*.
5 R. Nozick, *Anarchy, State and Utopia* (Oxford 1984), pp. 35 and 100.
6 Thomas Hobbes, *Leviathan* (Penguin Books, London 1968), p. 199.
7 'Maritime Law' in M. Elon (ed.), *Principles of Jewish Law* (Jerusalem 1975), p. 335.
8 G. E. M. Anscombe, 'On the Source of the Authority of the State', *Collected Papers III* (Oxford 1981), pp. 138 f.
9 Phillip Montague, 'Self defense and choosing between lives', *Philosophical Studies* 40, 1981.
10 Ibid.
11 G. P. Fletcher, 'Proportionality and the psychotic aggressor', *Israel Law Review* 8/3, 1973.

Chapter 9: Terrorism and Guerrilla War

1 My information about Mount Athos is from a Swan Hellenic lecture given by Canon Dennis Nineham.
2 C. A. J. Coady, 'The morality of terrorism', *Philosophy* 60/231, January 1985.

Chapter 10: Absolute Obligation

1 Most of these examples are taken from B. A. O. Williams, *Moral Luck* (Cambridge, 1976). William's own primary concern is not to rebut absolutist views of

obligation but rather to explore difficulties which he perceives in ethical cognitivism. However, his examples have been (widely) borrowed by others who produce them in discussion when attempting to refute absolutist theories.

Bibliography

Anon., *The Song of Roland* (trans. C. K. Scott-Moncrieff), University of Michigan Press, Ann Arbor 1959.

Anscombe, G. E. M., *Collected Papers* III, Oxford 1981.

Aquinas, *Summa Theologica* (Blackfriars and Eyre & Spottiswoode, London 1966), especially 2a2e, Q. 40, Q. 64, Q. 188 (vols 35, 38 and 47).

Augustine, *On the Sermon on the Mount* (Library of the Nicene and Post-Nicene Fathers vol. vi), Grand Rapids 1887.

—— *Contra Faustum* (*The Works of St Augustine*, vol. v trans. M. Dods,), Edinburgh 1872.

Beeler, J., *Warfare in Feudal Europe 730–1200*, New York 1971.

Best, Geoffrey, *Humanity in Warfare*, London 1980.

Brinton, H. H., *Quaker Journalists*, Pennsylvania 1972.

Brock, Peter, *Pacifism in the USA*, Princeton 1968.

—— *The Roots of War Resistance*, New York 1972.

—— *Pacifism in Europe to 1914*, Princeton 1972.

—— *Twentieth Century Pacifism*, New York, 1973.

Calvin, John, *Institutions of the Christian Church* (trans. F. L. Battles), London, 1961.

Coady, C. A. J., 'The Idea of Violence', *Journal of Applied Philosophy* vol. 3 no. 1, 1986.

—— 'The Morality of Terrorism', *Philosophy* 60/231, Jan. 1985.

—— 'Nuclear Intentions and Morality' (forthcoming).

Cowdrey, H. E. J., 'Bishop Ermenfried of Sion and the Penitential Ordinance following the Battle of Hastings', *Journal of Ecclesiastical History* 20, 1969.

—' The Peace of God', *Past and Present* 46, 1970.

Denyer, Nicholas, 'Just War', in Hide Ishiguro (ed.), *The Philosophy of G. E. M. Anscombe*, The Hague (forthcoming).

Dictionary of Moral Theology, London 1957.

Douglas, David C. (ed.)., *English Historical Documents*, Cambridge 1969.

Elon, Menachem (ed.), *Principles of Jewish Law*, Jerusalem 1975.

Flannery, Austin (ed.), *Vatican Council II*, Dublin 1974.

Fletcher, G.P., 'The right to life', *Monist*, 63, 1980.

—— 'Proportionality and the Psychotic Aggressor', *Israel Law Review* 8/3, 1973.

Garver, Newton, 'What Violence Is', in J. Rachels and F. A. Tillman (eds), *Philosophical Issues: A Contemporary Introduction*, New York 1972.

Grotius, Hugo, *De jure belli ac pacis* (trans. F. W. Kelsey), Oxford 1925.

Harris, John (ed.), *Violence and Responsibility*, London 1980.

Hobbes, Thomas, *Leviathan*, London 1968.

John XXIII, *Pacem in Terris*, Catholic Truth Society pamphlet, London.

Kant, Immanuel, *Perpetual Peace* (trans. M. Campbell Smith), London 1903.

Keeton, G. W., *Trial for Treason*, London 1959.

Montague, Phillip, 'Self defense and choosing between lives', *Philosophical Studies* 40, 1981.

National Conference of Catholic Bishops (of the USA), *The Challenge of Peace*, Chicago 1983.

New Catholic Encyclopedia, Washington, D.C. 1967.

Nozick, Robert, *Anarchy, State and Utopia*, Oxford 1984.

Origen, *Contra Celsum* (trans. Henry Chadwick), Cambridge 1953.

Roberts, A. and Guellf, R. (eds), *Documents on the Laws of War*, Oxford 1982.

Russell, F. H., *The Just War in the Middle Ages*, Cambridge 1975.

Shaw, G. B., *Prefaces*, London 1934.

Sharples, Isaac, *History of the Quaker Government in Pennsylvania*, Philadelphia 1900.

Sheils, W. J. (ed.), *The Church and War*, Oxford 1983.

Suarez, Francisco, *A Work on the Theological Virtues* (trans. G. L. Williams, Ammi Brown and John Waldron, revised by Henry Davis SJ), Oxford 1944.

Tertullian, *On Idolatry* (Ante-Nicene Christian Library: *Tertullian*), Edinburgh 1869.

Thomson, Judith Jarvis, 'Self Defense and Rights', Kansas 1976.

Uniacke, Suzanne M., 'The Doctrine of Double Effect', *The Thomist* 48, 1984.

Vipont, E., *The Story of Quakerism*, London 1954.

Vitorio, Francisco, *De Indis et de jure belli relectiones* (trans. J. P. Bate, edited by E. Nys), Washington, D.C. 1917.

Wasserstrom, Richard A. (ed.), *Morality and War*, California 1970.

Index

THE LIBRARY
ST. MARY'S COLLEGE OF MARYLAND.
ST. MARY'S CITY. MARYLAND 20686

AUG 1 8 1989